WELCOME

TO THE ARTIST'S GUIDE TO ILLUSTRATION

LEARN FROM THE WORLD'S BEST ILLUSTRATORS

Welcome to the second in our series of *Artist's Guides*, which provide a wealth of in-depth tutorials and features to help you produce your best art and designs ever. In *The Artist's Guide to Illustration*, many of the world's leading professional artists reveal the techniques and tricks that help them produce the

amazing works you'll find in these pages. You'll learn how to master the varied toolsets of Photoshop and Illustrator, and how to combine them with real-world crafts including pens, pencils and paints.

In this book you'll discover the secrets of a huge range of styles from hand-drawn to vector, and from portraits to type art.

To help you complete these tutorials, we've compiled their project files into a handy resource. There's far more than could possibly fit on a CD, so go to *theartistsguide.co.uk/ downloads* for quick access to the files.

The Artist's Guide to Illustration is your handbook to becoming the best illustrator you can be – so let's get started.

To discover how Alexandra Zutto created this image see page 80.

CONTENTS

INSIDE THE ARTIST'S GUIDE TO ILLUSTRATION

INSIDE

P54 MONTAGE TECHNIQUES

P76 TRACING TECHNIQUES

P88 BLACK-AND-WHITE ART

P80 LAYERING SKILLS

P90 QUIRKY VECTORS

P84 SECRETS OF CUTE

P94 LINES, SHAPES AND TEXTURES

CONTENTS

P104 CREATE VECTOR ART

P132 TILING TECHNIQUES

P110 VECTOR LIGHTING EFFECTS

P146 ILLUSTRATED LETTERING

P114 DYNAMIC ILLUSTRATOR

P150 TYPE-BASED GRAPHICS

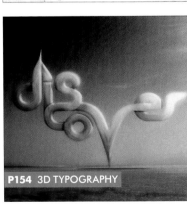

P124 REPEATING VECTOR PATTERNS

P128 CHEERY VECTORS

P158 FLUID TYPE EFFECTS

P154 3D TYPOGRAPHY

EDITORIAL
Editor Neil Bennett
neil_bennett@idg.co.uk
Art editor Johann Chan
johann_chan@idg.co.uk

With thanks to Rob Woodcock

ADVERTISING
Group advertising manager
James Poulson jamesp@idg.co.uk
Deputy group ad manager
Selen Sevket selen_sevket@idg.co.uk
Sales executive Rebecca Clewarth
rebecca_clewarth@idg.co.uk

Contact *Digital Arts* advertising
on 020 7756 2835

MARKETING
Assistant marketing manager
Emma van Beurden
emma_vanbeurden@idg.co.uk

PRODUCTION
Head of production Richard Bailey
richard_bailey@idg.co.uk
Deputy production manager
Fay Harward fay_harward@idg.co.uk

PUBLISHING
Editor-in-chief Mark Hattersley
mark_hattersley@idg.co.uk
Publishing director Mustafa Mustafa
mustafa@idg.co.uk
Managing director Kit Gould

PRODUCTION SERVICES
Printed by Wyndeham Group

SUBSCRIPTIONS/BACK ISSUES
Call the hotline on 01858 438 867

ADDRESS
101 Euston Road, London, NW1 2RA
Tel: 020 7756 2800
Fax (ads): 020 7756 2838

IDG COMMUNICATIONS recycle

CHAPTER 1

HAND-DRAWN TECHNIQUES

IMPROVE YOUR SKILLS WITH PENS, PENCILS & GRAPHICS TABLETS

"I like to use lines on the face, like an anatomical drawing. But some clients don't like this approach, so I have to limit the amount and weight of the lines – unfortunately," says Andy Macgregor.

Rediscover your love of drawing & see your art take flight. We speak to creatives who have a passion for the hand-fashioned

Top Drawer

Words: Alice Ross

Think back to the first time you wielded a pen, pencil or crayon. Drawing is one of the first ways children express themselves visually. A lucky few go on to hone and perfect their skills over decades, building their whole career on that simple pleasure of drawing a pen across paper – or graphics tablet – and marvelling at the result.

Once upon a time, it was simply impossible to be an artist, without having superb drawing skills. Sketching and drawing were the foundations on which paintings, carvings, frescos and sculptures were built. But that was then. In a digital era, it's easy to avoid ever having to pick up a pencil. Many stellar creative careers rest more on high-tech software and great source imagery, than on traditional art skills.

Why, when you can create dazzling work using Photoshop filters and intricate Illustrator line work, would you dedicate the time and energy to perfecting your drawing? After all, it's a skill that demands minute physical control, an understanding of media (if you're sketching on paper, you need to understand the different ways that pencils, charcoals, inks and crayons work) and endless, endless practice.

First, because it's fun. The ability to pick up a pen – whether you're working on paper or using a graphics tablet – and let your imagination take flight is exhilarating.

The act of drawing has a sense of playfulness that can take artists back to the intense concentration and experimentation of early childhood.

Second, because it's liberating. Artist Dave Bain (*davebain.com*) who creates everything from delicate mixed-media pieces to bright naïve paintings says, "There is something wonderfully immediate about using a pencil on paper, without having to switch on a computer screen or click a mouse."

> *"There is something wonderfully immediate about using a pencil on paper"*
> Dave Bain

Above far left
Sam de Buysscher advises, "Never ignore things you find hard to draw. Look at them as a challenge."

Above middle
Dave Bain's illustration for the Queensberry Hotel's Olive Tree Restaurant in Bath.

Above
Gemma Correll's ampersand design drawn for a Flickr photostream follower inspired her to create a letterpressed print of it to sell.

Right Sam Kerr says, "This self-initiated piece was derived from the opinion that Michael Jackson peaked at *Thriller*."

Far right Sam's portrait of John Lennon was part of a series created for a London wine bar. He says, "Each piece has a wine theme. In this case, Lennon's glasses are made using actual red wine marks."

Right Sam uses iPhone app Paint to sketch people on the go. He says, "It's the best practise for drawing portraits to achieve a likeness. You're restricted to what you can do with five brush sizes, a small screen and some fat fingers."

Far right Oliver Barrett's portraits of The Beatles are sold as prints. He says, "Constant learning, experimentation and exploration is the best and most obvious way to get better."

notable instruments of
RINGO STARR

Belgian illustrator Sam de Buysscher, who works under the name Toy Factory, says sketching on paper is liberating, both physically and mentally. "You get more freedom to draw wherever and whenever you want. Nothing is more fun than drawing in a park under a sunny sky. Nature can be your studio – isn't that great?"

There is also the fact that when you draw, even if you're using the very latest graphics tablet, you're tapping into a creative heritage that stretches back over centuries. This gives you an incredible archive of past masters to learn from and a dizzy range of styles and techniques to explore.

"I'm often looking through art books from the past. Classical drawing styles have always fascinated me, whether it's a rough, preliminary sketch, or a fully realised etching," says Dave Bain. These influences can clearly be traced in some of his work, such as the image of two brawling women (see page 9), immaculately rendered in a late-Victorian sketch style.

"Sketching on paper is liberating, both physically and mentally"
Sam de Buysscher

there is no fail-safe capturing a likeness"

Face facts

Drawing a face is simple enough. Drawing a portrait is another matter entirely. For a lucky few, comes naturally.

Andy Macgregor's portraits of actor Johnny Depp, rapper Common and others have appeared in many magazines. He says, "Portraits are my forte. As long as the reference image is of reasonable quality, it's pretty easy to achieve a likeness."

"Unfortunately, there is no fail-safe approach to capturing a likeness," says Sam Kerr, whose illustrations have featured rock stars, politicians and Osama Bin Laden. "I don't get it right all of the time. Some people are harder to draw than others. I've managed to make a very pretty friend look a little mannish on several occasions."

His advice is, "Make sure you really look at your subject. Get to know their face before you draw it."

Sam adds that the best portraits go beyond mere facial features. "I love the challenge of capturing not only a likeness, but also something of the person's character."

Oliver Barrett's portraits of jazz greats and The Beatles have been made into poster series. He says, "I find relaxing and trying to get a likeness in the early stages of the drawing helps. I've often overworked eyes or lips, then not got the instant recognition that I'm after. If it's not working, I will usually just erase the problem area and start over."

Left "I like to draw quickly sometimes, which means you have to sacrifice accuracy for a more energetic, looser sketch. This has its own unique quality to it," says Andy Macgregor.

Honing your drawing skills doesn't have to mean turning your back on digital art. Many creatives find the two work perfectly, hand in hand, offering the chance to combine the spontaneous feel of sketches with the flexibility of digital working and the all-important **Cmd/Ctrl + Z**.

Mixing it up

Illustrator Sam Kerr's works (*debutart.com/artist/sam-kerr*) combine beautifully observed drawings and paintings with crisp vector images.

"Hand-drawn stuff is very final. Once it's done, you've got to be happy with it, or start again," he says. "Combining digital [elements] allows room for adjustment within your image. In the same manner, the graphic elements allow me to be more creative with ideas as drawing in detail from photographs can have its restrictions."

Andy Macgregor's (*andymacgregor.com*) portraits and illustrations have appeared in *The Guardian* and *GQ*. He says integrating hand drawings with software is especially useful when working for clients.

"It gives me the freedom I need to produce exactly what is asked of me. Time lines are very tight and clients tend to change their minds a lot, so I have to be able to amend the illustration quickly and easily."

He adds, "It also means I can experiment and find the best solution to the problem."

Dave Bain says, "I sometimes use Photoshop to manipulate the drawing in ways that are not achievable or time-consuming to accomplish non-digitally. An example is using several scanned-in textures I've created using experimental techniques. I'll then tweak these using the Contrast and Levels settings, before incorporating them into artwork I've drawn out."

Meanwhile, other artists work entirely digitally, using techniques adopted wholesale from hand drawing. Oliver Barrett (*oliverbarrett.com*) combines his day job at US graphic design and branding agency Go Media with a sideline in lush portraits of musicians and other luminaries. He says his graphics tablet, rather than pen or pencil, is his key creative tool.

Playtime with Toy Factory

"I needed more dynamic characters. That is when I started sketching again". Sam de Buysscher

As the name of his one-man studio, Toy Factory, suggests, Belgian illustrator Sam de Buysscher's work is playful and slightly kitsch. It draws on the 1940s and 50s to create bright, fun works filled with robots, zeppelins and monsters. A late bloomer to hand drawing, Antwerp-based Sam admits this added a new lease of life to his work.

"In the beginning, I worked directly in Illustrator – no sketching, no scanning, just my mouse and Mac. Illustrator's borders are wide, but I wanted to create a more 'trashy' style; I needed more dynamic characters. That's when I started sketching again, and rediscovered my love for drawing. It has taken my work to another level."

Sketching has quickly become the starting point for almost all his images. "You get a whole other look to your work when you first make sketches. When I'm creating new characters and need to place them in different positions, it's handy to draw them first – you get a clearer image."

For Sam, rediscovering drawing is part of an ongoing urge to experiment. "It's part of my freedom and not getting stuck in a specific style."

He adds, "Lately I've started to get invitations for live drawing sessions, something I would never have done a few years ago."

toyfactory.be

Above Sam de Buysscher says, "Robots are fun to draw. They always have kind of magic and people keep on loving them."

Right AtomBoy is a character created by Sam. "At the moment I'm totally in love with my AtomBoy character," he says. "I could go on drawing it forever. It's a lovely mixture of characters and objects."

Oliver explains, "Usually I will do a rough thumbnail sketch, in order to get a basic idea of what the composition will be. From there, it depends on the project. There's always a lot of graphics tablet work, but occasionally I do work on paper extensively and then scan it in. After that, I may use scanned in textures and layering techniques to achieve the result I'm after."

In contrast, award-winning illustrator Gemma Correll (*gemmacorrell.com*) works predominantly on paper. "It's all hand drawn," she says of her blocky, childlike illustration style. "I sometimes add colour digitally, but the line work is always done by hand. I have tried drawing with my graphics tablet but it didn't really work for me – the line quality wasn't right."

She continues, "I enjoy the freedom of mark making and experimenting with media. I find felt pens and markers

easy to use. If I make mistakes, I might erase them later using Photoshop – or I might leave them in. Sometimes think mistakes add to the character of an illustration."

Learning to draw can be a long, hard process – and it's one that's never finished. Even the most skilled artists have objects they struggle to draw. But all this can be overcome with two simple techniques: observation and practice.

Be quick on the draw

Dave Bain claims the secret is to keep drawing and looking. "Wherever I am, if I have the materials to do it, I'll try to do a drawing," he says. "Even if I'm not quite in the mood or the final result is weak, just that process of drawing keeps me focused and improves my ability."

Dave adds that he sketches a lot when he's out and about. "If I'm drawing in public I tend to look at the people

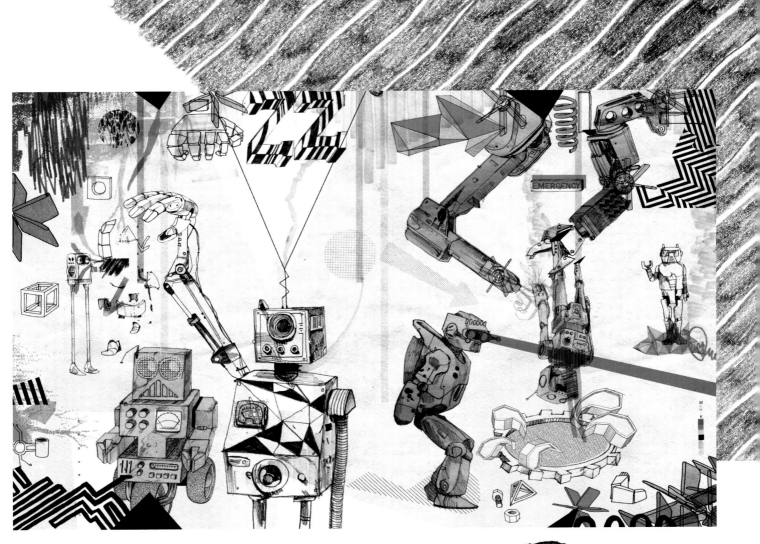

and not at the drawing page. I do fast, quick drawings that give me an impression of the movement of the person, rather than spot-on accuracy."

He says these sketches often get recycled into his other work. "I find that when I draw, all kinds of ideas flood into my mind about how that drawing can be used, or other ideas that I'd like to try out."

Andy Macgregor says, "I try to use the old-fashioned [method of] looking at the reference constantly, ghosting in the shape of whatever it is I'm drawing, then running the final line on top."

He continues, "It's most definitely a practice thing, but you should never be afraid to just draw what you see and welcome a sense of naïvety to your work."

Andy admits finding drawing most challenging when he can't base his drawings on observation.

"The most difficult thing to draw is something you have to pluck out of your mind. Sometimes, there's no reference for what you're asked to draw." He says in these situations you have to completely rely on your common sense and give way to trial and error.

While Andy can draw some things without observing them, Sam Kerr finds others extremely challenging.

"Don't ever ask me to draw a cow from memory," he says. "However, like with anything that you might struggle to draw, the best approach is to keep at it, until you get it right."

As with any artistic discipline, constantly experimenting with materials and techniques is an essential part of honing your skills and developing your style. Indeed, Andy reveals one of the simplest tricks is also one of the most effective.

"Be confident in your own ability," he says. "Everybody is different. You've got to nurture the skills you have and be confident doing it."

Above
Andy Macgregor's *El Bot* for *El Bosque*, a Colombian illustration magazine. "Everything is hand-drawn first, then all other elements are added separately – paint washes, found paper scans and mark making."

Right *The Guardian* commissioned this piece from Sam Kerr. "The column it supported spoke of Gordon Brown's dual personality, comparing him to Dr Jekyll and Mr Hyde."

Handy advice

Ask any 10 artists what they find hardest to draw, and at least seven of them will say 'hands'. With their tricky proportions and all that detail, they're certainly fiddly. But how to get them right?

"Draw them larger and bonier than usual – like Egon Schiele," says Andy Macgregor, referring to the Austrian 20th-Century painter. "Naturally, people tend to draw hands too small and make them look like a plastic doll's – not a good look."

Hands are a motif of Dave Bain's artwork. "I've been drawing hands since I was in my teens," he says. "I would often draw during lectures or in school. Hands are immediate and could be held in so many positions. In a way it was therapeutic."

The good thing about hands is that you can practice drawing them anywhere. "Try to make a lot of sketches of your own hands in different positions, and do this as much as you can – you will get better at it," recommends Sam de Buysscher.

Oliver Barrett agrees that practice is essential. "One of my teachers got me over the hump by forcing me to draw them over and over again, and from all kinds of different angles."

Right "It's so important to enjoy and be excited about drawing," says Dave Bain. "Even if the subject matter you are working on is dark in nature and that's the mood you're in."

Below Dave's minutely observed drawings of hands are usually modelled on his own or his friends' hands.

"Draw them larger an bonier than usual – like Egon Schiele

Andy Macgregor

STEP 12 Once the piece is fully coloured, open up *dots.eps* in Illustrator from the project and copy and paste all of the dots into your

Photoshop document to give a halftone effect. If you don't have Illustrator, you can Place the EPS into Photoshop, but copy and pasting will maintain it as a vector for smoother results after resizing.

Choose how intense you would like the dots to be. I picked the mid purple that I used throughout the project, which keeps them quite subtle. I coloured them using a Colour Overlay. This can be done by double clicking on the dots layer in the layer palette.

STEP 13 The piece is nearly complete. But the icing on the psychedelic cake are some final effects. Save yourself out a copy of the PSD for future editing if needed, then merge all colour layers and any other layer except for the overlaying clouds and spikes – keep these as separate layers for now.

Go to **Filter > Blur > Gaussian Blur** and give this new layer a blur of around 0.5 pixels. This just softens the linework up a little. Merge all your layers.

STEP 14 Add a Levels Adjustment layer and tweak the colours a little to make sure they are as rich as they can be. Select all, copy and paste. Set this new layer's blending mode to Soft Light and turn the opacity down to around 40%. Also add a Gaussian Blur of two pixels to this layer.

STEP 15 Flatten all artwork to a single layer. Now duplicate this layer and use a Gaussian Blur set to 4.8 pixels on the new layer.

STEP 16 Select a soft, large Eraser brush (**E**) and begin to erase the blurred layer, taking care to leave areas of blur, particularly around the edges. This helps to give the art a more floaty, dreamy, soft focus-type look. ■

PROFILE OLLIE MUNDEN

> Ollie Munden – aka Megamunden – is an illustrator whose work combines nature's creatures, tattoo design, psychedelia, 1980s skate graphics and an essence of the Far East to create his illustrations.

CONTACT
• *megamunden.com*

Above top A poster to promote the Croatian Garden music festival. Ollie says: "I used a lot of digital painting in Photoshop on this artwork, something I don't normally do. I found some great brushes in the Wet Brush palette that gave some realistic results"

Above "This piece was a collaboration with VelvetSpectrum (*velvetspectrum. com*). VS has been learning 3D software and wanted to use some of my character illustrations as inspiration to create 3D characters. It was used for PlayStation's new theme store called The Studio. (*uk.playstation.com/thestudio*)"

Create iconic T-shirt artwork

Use Illustrator to draw a biker-style graphic using vector shapes

> **INFO**

TIME TO COMPLETE
• 4 hours

SOFTWARE
• Adobe Illustrator & Photoshop CS3

PROJECT FILES
• Files for this tutorial are downloadable from *theartistsguide.co.uk/ downloads*

oshua Smith, aka maverick illustrator Hydro74, has a style that's instantly recognisable – combining the thick, clean lines of graffiti with the iconography of tattoos and the symmetry and patterns of vector art. Here he takes you through how he created this work, based around his regular motifs of skulls and swirls mixed with an owl.

As you follow this tutorial, you'll discover lots of tricks to help you create better art and work faster in Illustrator. You'll learn how to improve your skills with line art, shading using flat fills

and colour techniques for limited palettes (to keep printing costs down).

Joshua says that as his techniques are more about drawing vector shapes using the Pen tools than brush strokes, you'll get better results from a mouse than a graphics tablet. Joshua adds that he wrote this tutorial using Illustrator CS3, as he finds the Pathfinder tool – which features a lot in this tutorial – in CS4 to be painful when dealing with complex paths.

Joshua has also kindly provided us with a wealth of vector artworks and fonts, available in the project files.

"Don't follow your lines directly from the drawing, but allow yourself to be free – you're doing this to explore."

01 First off, I did a really rough drawing of the head of an owl to get the piece in motion. Then I went into Photoshop and made it symmetrical. The goal here with a rough, basic drawing is to allow yourself to be more creative in Illustrator as you click away. You never just want to trace what is there, but add your touch on what feels right and allow that inner creative demon to ask: 'What if we did this?'. You can use your own sketch here, or open *Owl. ai* from the project files.

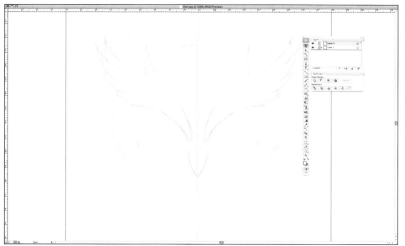

02 Import your image into Illustrator, enlarge it to a decent size and drop the transparency down to 50%. From there, set up a guide in the centre of the image. The goal is to save time, thus drawing one side and perfecting that. Create a new layer to allow you to click off the drawing to see how progress is going.

03 Now it's time to click and drag using the Pen tool (**P**). As you click away, start adding small amounts of detail and exploring what works. Don't follow your lines directly from the drawing, but allow yourself to be free – you're doing this to explore.

04 When you get to a good spot, copy the art and flip it. Once I put the two sides together, I can see where my mistakes are, or if I'm on target. This is a good point to step away for a few moments and get a cup of tea, so you can look at the piece with fresh eyes.

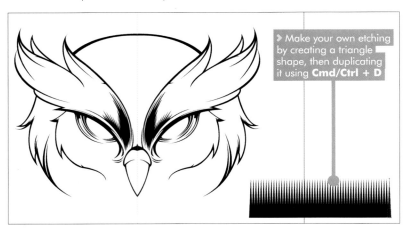

> Make your own etching by creating a triangle shape, then duplicating it using **Cmd/Ctrl + D**

05 Once you've drawn the outline, it's time to add some details. I've worked a little etching into the piece by creating long, thin triangle-shaped pieces arranged together in a row.

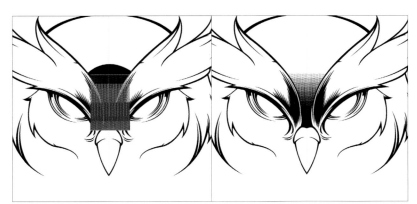

06 Take the etching element and play with it by stretching it then placing it over the owl's eyebrows. To funnel it between the eyebrows, select the element, open the Pathfinder (**Shift + Cmd/Ctrl + F9**) and use the Crop function. One downside to this function is that every time you crop, you'll notice annoying blank lines. To remove them, use the Pen tool to make a line with no colour or stroke, then click on **Select > Same > Fill & Stroke**. Hit **Delete** and you're done. Keep a copy of the etching lines nearby.

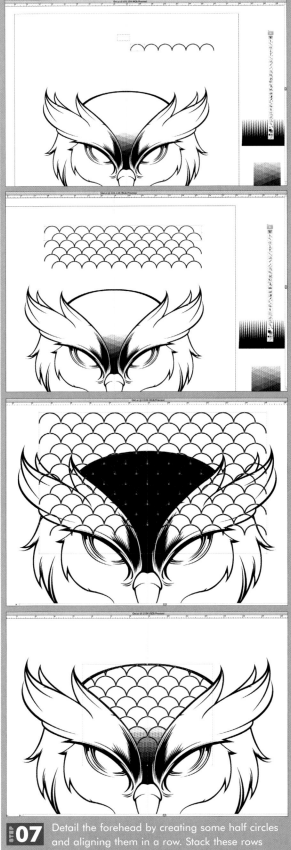

07 Detail the forehead by creating some half circles and aligning them in a row. Stack these rows to cover the area that you want to fill. It helps to group (**Cmd/Ctrl + G**) these shapes before placing them on top of the illustration so you don't have to click them individually if you make a mistake.

SAVE IT FOR LATER

➤ As you are working on an illustration, always make a copy on the side so you can use it again if you need to — especially if, like me, you love to crop things down. This is because you never know when you may want to grab an element for a future piece — or go back to it to remove the eyeball nipples.

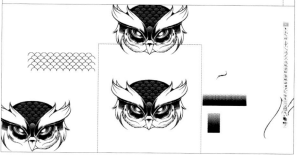

STEP 08 Repeat the techniques from Step 6 to add etching to these 'feathers' (this is why I told you to keep a copy of those etching lines.) You can fill each half-circle separately, or fill the whole section with this element to save time. I've decided to do each one individually, as it looks better.

STEP 10 Now for some detail. This is a good point to start filling in areas with black, and adding little texture scrapes. The goal is to make it look somewhat organic. At this point, I also like to start deleting things I don't need, but I don't want to lose anything I worked on in case I change my mind. Create a copy, drag it to the top and you're free to experiment without worry.

STEP 09 To fill each half-circle individually, duplicate the cropped element you just created, rather than cropping each area. Once done filling those areas, select each one and crop it into the head. If you want to experiment here, try using wider or smaller shapes, or halftone dots.

STEP 11 Add some feathers at the sides, flowing downwards to tie in the body elements. They also fill out the artwork's dimensions to better suit a T-shirt print. I want to put a skull under the head, but if skulls aren't your thing, add a fluffy little cloud, or a happy little tree, or something. ➤

12 If you have a Hydro74 trademarked skull handy, feel free to use it now. Custom typography would work well here, too. Drop in the skull and start building the surrounding areas. It's starting to come together a little now.

13 Section off the different components – the owl and the skull – as individual elements. To do this, group together the owl head and trace around it in white. Repeat with the skull. This way, you can resize those elements more easily.

14 Since you have the two heads filled in, start dropping in some highlights and dark areas onto one of the wings to add detail. Play around with some etching elements and send them to the back, behind the owl head and skull. To detail the other wing, take the side you worked on, duplicate it and flip it. Finally for the outline, add some eyes to the skull. Try to ignore the fact that your owl now has eyeballs for nipples.

15 Time to add colour. This is the hard part, but here's a trick: create a line-art version of your artwork under the 'etched' one, so you can fill the parts without fiddling with the shading. To do this, place a large rectangle over the top and select Crop in the Pathfinder palette. Delete all blank fills and strokes. Lock down everything except the current piece. Click **Cmd/Ctrl + Shift + D** for a transparent background. Select a piece of white in your illustration, then click **Select > Same > Fill Color** and delete it. All that's left should be the black. Merge it together. Now create a new layer and place it under your line art. Lock the line art layer.

16 To fill out the print and make it seem more iconic, I've added some organic swirls and shapes around the main design. ■

Below & bottom
Joan of Arc and
Discover a Muse, by
Michael C Hayes.

Peter James Field graduated in 2005 from the University of Brighton with a degree in illustration. His clients include the BBC and many leading newspapers and magazines.

To generate ideas, Field will often start by juxtaposing different bits of reference material or pre-existing sketches and textures. "Very often I start with a collage, sometimes digital, sometimes analogue, which I then draw from using traditional materials. I also do lots of very straightforward naturalistic sketches from my own reference photos or, where possible, from direct observation."

His work is completely hand-drawn, but digital processes figure highly. "When I scan the collaged reference material, I often make big changes to the contrast or colours of the original sketch before it's suitable to send to a client," he says. "Sometimes I spend many hours in Photoshop cleaning up and perfecting the appearance of a sketch. Often I also digitally combine several drawn elements or background textures."

Working from reference pictures does have its drawbacks, he says. "Some sitters would be insulted to have their own personal uniqueness edited, whereas others may expect flattery as a matter of course. Asking before you start can save a lot of trouble later on."

"There are so many variations of grey tones."

When Italian artist Oscar Diadoro (*odd-house.com*) is commissioned to do a portrait, he works from a photo while first sketching on paper to study the composition. "Once I'm satisfied, I digitise the sketch and start retracing it," he explains. "I put the source image in a layer and reduce the opacity to 50 per cent. This helps me to distinguish the lines from the image itself. While retracing with the Pen tool, I work in outline view to have the background image always visible.

"I work only with strokes to 'ink' the illustration at first, then outline the strokes to work on details and smooth lines. Once I've got the black-and-white version, I start colouring. Every colour is set in a separate layer and I use the colour swatches in Global mode, so I can adjust or change colours without selecting every shape individually."

Illustrator Peter James Field (*peterjamesfield.co.uk*) uses pencil, colour pencils or paint for his portraits or figure pieces, although digital processes in Photoshop are also very important to the development and delivery of his art.

Working mainly from photos for his commercial art, he acknowledges that producing a drawn portrait from a photographic reference can be a challenge. "I always start by looking carefully at the reference picture, converting it to greyscale and making sure that there's a good contrast ❯

Above *Tourists* and *John*, by Peter James Field.

VINCENT BAKKUM'S ALTINAÏ

Altinaï, an acryclic-on-canvas work, is based on a photo Vincent Bakkum took "ages ago". The 140 x 140cm painting sold almost immediately when first exhibited.

The subject "resembles a Montenegrin princess in exile I met years ago at a party in Paris", says Bakkum. "Her name was Altinaï. A name for a mythological lady."

1 "First I drew her [based on the photograph], gave her some highlights and was very pleased with the composition and her looks, but I needed to add drama to the backdrop."

2 "Since I can't paint landscapes – my brushes turn all panoramas into pea soup – nor interiors, nor sports cars or racehorses, I always need some kind of 'wallpaper' to finish a painting."

3 "I borrowed some floral elements from a Dutch master. The beauty and serenity of these flowers behind her give her something untouchable."

4 "The soil I grew up in was Catholic, so I made her a saint. The gold leaf gave even more stature to her presence."

5 "A bird design on her dress, and *Altinaï* was ready to be shown to wherever I was taking her."

Above, left to right
Guilty and *Silvia* by Oscar Diodoro; *Somebody* and Ronnie Corbett by Peter James Field.

▶ between the lightest areas of the face and the shaded areas.

"I'll alter the contrast to make the facial features stand out, using a shade range between pure white and very dark grey," he continues. "I also make sure that all areas of the photo reference are visible.

"For example, sometimes the contrast on the face is perfect, but the person has dark hair against a dark background and the texture of the hair isn't really visible. I'll lasso that particular section of the photo and tweak the contrast of that specific bit."

For fleshing out a portrait, Finnish artist Minni Havas (*pekkafinland.fi/minnihavas*) recommends starting from your faintest colours and carefully adding them from lighter to darker on top of each other. "That way you can still make corrections to the image while drawing," she explains. "When I draw or paint skin, I keep in mind that human skin is translucent and covers blue and reddish blood vessels. So the skin isn't monotone.

"I never use black for shadows on skin or textile," she adds. "Instead I use complementary colours mixed with darker shades of the base hue."

Cardiff-based illustrator Kath Morgan (*kafine-ated.net*) uses a technique of working upwards through the levels of detail for both digital painting and acrylic. "What this means is that I'll start out by blocking in the main areas of light, dark and colour, making sure that all

"Keep in mind that human skin is translucent and covers blue and reddish blood vessels. It isn't monotone"
MINNI HAVAS

PROFILE AND PROCESS
MINNI HAVAS

Minni Havas studied fashion design at the University of Art and Design Helsinki in Finland, and has been a commercial illustrator for three years. Her portraits begin with her sketching the composition, she says. "I then collect photos for the montage I am going to make, especially if it is a whole-body image. I take a hand from one image, a face from another, and the hair from somewhere else. I basically create a new picture that resembles the one I have in mind. I make my drawing based on the montage I made. I then scan the finished drawing and join the parts together."

"The picture is most likely to lose its delicate shades when I scan it, so I try to restore the authenticity of the colouring digitally. In some cases I merge patterns and structures from the original photograph to the drawing. My goal, though, is always to keep the feeling that the picture is completely hand-drawn."

It's also essential to choose the right paper, she adds. "I use paper that is quite soft but not textured, and acid-free, 90g up to 130g."

Above, left to right Two pieces of personal work by Minni Havas, both done with watercolour pencils.

Above, far right image by Annelie Carlström for the Swedish fashion label Minimarket, which appeared on playing cards given away with their clothing.

the structures are as I want them," she explains. "Then I'll refine these with smaller brushes during the longest part of the painting process.

"The details go in last. Getting caught up in detail too early can result in a distorted image you can't bear to erase, or boredom when you realise how much work is left to go."

Vincent, for his part, starts with a white canvas. "I cover it with a couple of layers of transparent colours and half the work is done. A lot of the skin will be made out of the underlying colour. A beautiful trick born out of laziness, but it works."

For working on the face, it seems there as many techniques as there are human expressions. "It's important to get the shape of the face right first,"

says Stanley Chow (*stanleychow. co.uk*). "If you get that wrong, it's very hard to put the eyes, nose and mouth in the right place in relation with each other." That partly explains why Stanley's favourite features in Illustrator, or at least those he uses the most, include the Alignment panel and the Reflect tool.

Peter views the face as the sum of its parts. "They all interconnect," he says. "A smiling face will affect the light and shade on the cheeks or the lines round the eyes.

"With this in mind, I tend to build up shade quite slowly in layers, working on lots of areas of the face simultaneously." He says this helps unify the tones and lets every element blend into the next.

Minni advises that you spend time on building up textures on across the face and hair. "For example, eyeballs are covered with fluid and mouth is soft but wrinkly. Think about the face as a 3D object and draw the strokes according to the shape."

It's not necessary – or even possible – to replicate every single detail in a face, and adding too many lines may give a messy look. "I start by reducing details until I get the very essence of the face," says Oscar. "I try to be tight with the black ink, because I adjust and complete the details of the expression with lights and shadows."

"A little light in an eye does wonders," notes Anje Jager, while Peter tries to make the eyes a focal point by always leaving the whites ▶

SCHIN LOONG'S THE ROSE EATER

"This is the first in my series of *Eater* paintings," says Schin Loong. "I wanted to create a very opulent, grand view and collected many inspirations to create the final image.

"Most of my work these days is digital, although I incorporate traditional watercolour textures once in a while. I use mainly Photoshop and Corel Painter."

1 "A tiny drop of highlight and colour in the eyes goes a long way in brightening up the expression."

2 "Next to the face, the hand is the most expressive part of the body. Unfortunately, all those fingers and little joints make it quite difficult to do. I practise a lot by drawing my own hand whenever I have free time and studying beautiful hands and how the fingers, nails and palm curve."

3 "Here I used a lot of textures, but kept her skin marble-smooth as a contrast."

4 "Flowers bring femininity [to a piece], and the type of flower will shape the viewer's subconscious feeling for the portrait, too. Roses bring a particular feeling of luxury and passion."

Above & far right
Schin Loong's *Butterfly Kisses* and *The Moth Eater.*

perfectly white. "If you look at a photo of a face, the brow often casts some shadow over the whites of the eyes," he says. "By keeping them white, though, you can add a little extra impact."

According to Stanley, the eyebrows are the most important area in capturing an expression. "Like the human face, the eyes pretty much stay the same shape; it's eyebrows that help create an expression.

"You can say a lot with the position of the eyebrow in relation to the eye," he explains. "The higher the eyebrow, the more of a surprised look is achieved; the lower it is, the more of a scowl you get. Having one eyebrow higher than the other creates a cheeky expression."

Paying attention to lighting and composition can also give a portrait impact. "Using the flow of hair, lines or objects, I try to direct the viewer's eye to the face," says Schin. "This can also be done using colour gradation or just manipulating the space around it. I try to keep it so there is no dead space in my painting and [there's] always something interesting to look at, even if it is just flat colour."

FLATTERING ANGLES
A head-on face-to-face pose is best for capturing the whole face but, according to Peter, a low angle is less favourable if you're going for flattery, as it will accentuate the chin and neck. "For me the ideal facial pose is three-quarters," he says. "A half-turn

of the head looks slightly less formal, less passport photo-ish and also shows off the nose slightly better."

Painter Michael C Hayes (*artofmike.com*) feels you can get good poses, movement, expressions and a sense of life by combining two things. The first is to build "a visual library and an aesthetic sense, through experience and practice, of what works well visually".

Michael says that when you draw from observation and you see something that jumps out at you as extraordinary – from the twist of a

dancer's body to the subtle parting of a person's lips – you should make a note of it in your head.

His second piece of advice is obtain a good selection of reference materials for the particular expression or pose that you want for your piece.

"A good camera, lighting and model will pay dividends," he says. "You use the photo reference to fill in the gaps of your memory, and you use your memory, experience and aesthetic sense to improve upon or deviate from your reference where it falls short."

Michael likes to use a main light source. "Even when I add in secondary light, I make sure to keep one [source] dominant," he says. "From there it is a matter of physics: no area in the shadow can be brighter than the areas in light. It sounds simple, yet so many artists really struggle with it."

Peter feels that good directional lighting – where one light source is cast against one side of the face – is preferable. "A light source above will cast shadows over the eyes and may create problems in getting a hold of the likeness," he says.

Another common issue is keeping the proportions consistent, particularly if the figure is standing.

"You can easily end up with big feet and a tiny head," advises Kath Morgan. "On paper, tilt your image so that it's in line with your face, and your eye will stop trying to compensate for perspective. Digitally, make sure you look at your sketch ▶

Top, left to right
Fascinator and *Persephone* by Kath Morgan; Paul Nizon by Anje Jager, for the German magazine *Intersection*.

Above, left to right
Princesita and *Yes, You!* by Vincent Bakkum.

THE ART OF EXAGGERATION

Caricatures exaggerate or distort the essence of their subject. They're often used to depict politicians and celebrities, so it is key to ensure that caricatures do look like their subjects.

"Once the likeness has been achieved," says illustrator Stanley Chow (*stanleychow.co.uk*), "then it's down to deciding whether I want to just concentrate on the head and shoulders or [go for] a full-length pose," he says.

"The caricatures I do are essentially portraits done in my style; they only really become a caricature when I add a small body, thus exaggerating the size of the head."

Stanley feels that a caricature can become "just cheesy" if based on a clumsy exaggeration of the features. Which features you exaggerate, and by how much, determines whether you stay on the right side of cheesy, he says. For his part, he usually chooses to accentuate the girth of the neck or the shape of the face.

Illustrator Sam Kerr (*bit.ly/iiqdJZ*) produces humorous images that often stray into caricature. A prime example is his depiction for *GQ* magazine of musician Jack White playing a cloud-and-lightning guitar (*top right*). "The image was for a feature on White's new band, The Dead Weather," says Kerr. "The idea evolved from using weather as a theme, not just because of the band's name, but also White's shifting allegiance to different bands which, wait for it, changes like the weather!

"It's important to capture a likeness, but for me the emphasis is on the idea, no matter how small or stupid," he continues. "If you can get your point across in an interesting way, the rest is easy-ish."

▶ zoomed right out from time to time, and flip it often."

Peter will also often work by turning both his sketch and the original reference sideways or upside down. "This can work by helping the logical side of your brain to forget you're drawing 'an eye' or 'a nose'," he says. "If you can start to view the portrait as an abstraction of light and shade, it will be more truthful."

Helsinki-based Miika Saksi (*miikasaksi.com*) has some unconventional advice for creating the best portraits. "Lie," he says. "If you are doing a portrait of a person who doesn't look interesting or working from a photo that has imperfections, you don't have to be compliant with the original image. You can make eyes bigger and brighter, the chin stronger, teeth whiter and cleaner, features symmetrical, and so on.

"Make the person look interesting and awesome, because you can. It doesn't have to be so truthful. It's your vision."

Schin disagrees, preferring to try to find perfection in imperfection. "A face that is too beautiful and perfect can be ugly or just plain weird," she says. "Nobody's face is perfectly symmetrical.

"First I try to make the face as beautiful as I can, then sometimes I purposely make it cockeyed or the eyes slightly asymmetrical. As long as the face looks right, I don't really worry too much about being 100 per cent anatomically accurate." ∎

> "First I try to make the face as beautiful as I can, then sometimes I purposely make it cockeyed"
> SCHIN LOONG

Above top Jack White by Sam Kerr.

Above middle Wayne Rooney by Stanley Chow.

Above (left to right) Nina Simone, Gwyneth Paltrow as Margot Tenenbaum, and Bill Murray, all by Stanley Chow.

12 To create the environment, begin making little elements such as grass, plants and stones. Draw several grass shapes and fill them with different gradients, using transparency to make them look as though they're shrouded in fog. Copy groups of grass to save time. Fill in the background with similar elements, making distant layers lighter.

13 The next step is adding a light source. In tundra, the light is pale and scattered. So make a simple circle and fill it with Light Radial gradient. Make the outer colour of the gradient fully transparent. Adjust the gradient sliders to give softness to the sun's shape. Use this technique to make small particles and distribute them over the picture.

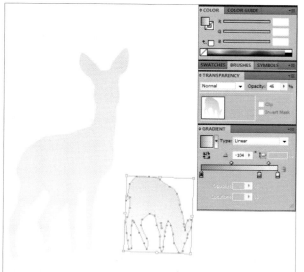

14 If you want to add some other creatures such as deer in the background, find some pictures of them, and outline their shape and place them in the background.

15 To give a sense of magic, I've added some rainbows. Make some round shapes and fill them with a gradient that consists of some bright colours in the centre and is transparent inside and outside. Vary the transparency of them between 10-50%.

16 Now we need to add some finishing touches to the picture. Create some shapes in the same way as you made the sun, but in different colours. Make them nearly transparent and place them on the picture where you want to add some additional soft light. ∎

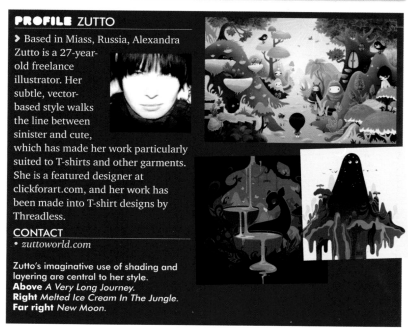

> **LEARN** VECTOR DRAWING

Create a hip, cute character

Bubblefriends-creator Sascha Preuß teaches the art of designing colourful cartoon characters and reveals the principles of cuteness

"Oh how cute!" When this exclamation is heard from someone viewing an illustration by Sascha Preuß – aka Bubblefriends – he knows he's created another winning piece.

Sascha says that creating cute figures requires neither supernatural powers nor rare talents – it isn't that difficult if you follow a core set of principles. Here he reveals the rules of cuteness – plus how to stay the right side of the line between cutely hip and childishly schmaltzy. Step by step, Sascha will take you through the development of a character from the first sketch to the final colouring.

"Our small character is a can of bug spray who frightens every kind of insect with his little cloudy friend," says Sascha. "Together they put the evil guys to flight. Cute but pitiless!"

CHARACTER BUILDING

> It all begins with a pencil drawing. The accurateness of the sketch contributes to the success of a vector illustration. Problems like shading, plasticity or composition can be solved in the sketching process, so take your time. Don't start your digital work until after the pencil drawing is completed.

03 Scan in your sketch (or use mine from the project files). Open Illustrator and select **File > New** (or hit **Cmd/Ctrl + N**) to create a new document. Select an A4 portrait size and CMYK colour mode. Set Raster Effects to High (300 ppi).

Import your sketch using **File > Place**. Go to the Layers panel and create a new layer. Lock the 'sketch' layer. The Pen and Ellipse tools and the Pathfinder panel are your main tools. Over the next steps, we'll be tracing the shapes using a stroke of 0.25pt with rounded caps and corners. We're just doing the linework and blocking out the shaded areas that represent shadows first – colours will be added after all the shapes are completed.

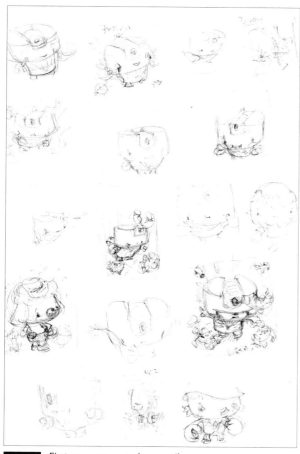

01 First, use paper and a pencil to try out some possible character designs and poses. At the beginning your sketches should be fast and fleet – then allow the characters to develop later. From my point of view, it's not necessarily required to have a story in mind before sketching.

Select one of your designs and develop your sketches, making them more accurate and precise.

> To make your character cute, think about the proportions of a baby and exaggerate the character's childlike features

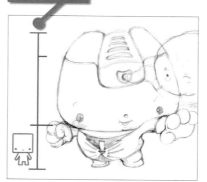

02 What is cute? Cute has something of the 'newborn' about it – as without help, newborns cannot survive. Looking at a baby activates protective instincts, and it's the awakening of those instincts that usually identifies something as cute.

Cute comes from the childlike arrangement of characteristics. The size of the head is important, as in comparison to other body parts it grows slowly. For optimum cuteness, we must exaggerate and draw a head that's half the size of the whole body height.

> **INFO**

TIME TO COMPLETE
• 4 hours

SOFTWARE
• Adobe Illustrator CS 2 or later

PROJECT FILES
• Files for this tutorial are downloadable from *theartistsguide.co.uk/downloads*

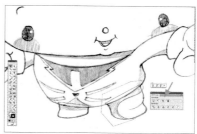

04 The legs should be short and fat so that the figure appears to be clumsy and lazy. Passivity and an impression of helplessness further brings out our protective instinct and ups the 'cute' factor.

First, draw a leg with the Pen tool (**P**), then add an area for shading in a way that they overlap each other. Select the leg, copy it and paste a duplicate in front of the original (**Cmd/Ctrl + C**, then **Cmd/Ctrl + F**). Break up the elements into separate areas by selecting them all then clicking on Divide in the Pathfinder panel. ➤

> "Keep your character simple, as too many details spoil the picture. The body should appear soft and round – baby fat is cute!"

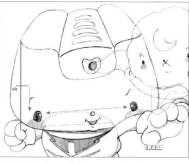

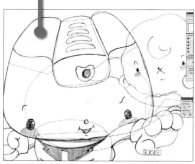

> The best way to create rounded elements within others is to draw ellipses with the Ellipse tool, then draw the area you want to cut out of it. Then use the Pathfinder panel to subtract the latter from the former.

09 An adult's eyes sit almost in the middle of the head vertically, but a baby's are very low down comparatively. Here, the eyes should be positioned almost at the bottom of the face and sit far apart.

Babies also have big eyes compared to an adult – so should our character.

Draw each eye and cheek with the Ellipse tool (**L**). Duplicate and flip them with the Reflect tool (**O**).

05 Draw an ellipse circling the neck with the Pen tool. Then create the torso. Keep it simple, as too many details spoil the picture. Impressive muscles won't fit in. The body should appear soft and round (baby fat is cute). Leave out the foremost arm – it will be added after the head is drawn.

07 Draw the outline of the whole head with the Pen tool, then add overlapping kidney-shaped outlines to create the three parts of the forehead. Use the same Duplicate-then-Divide process as in Step 4 to break them into separate elements.

Repeat the procedure for the rest of the linework within the head.

10 Draw eyebrows with the Ellipse and the Knife tools – just draw a whole circle then cut off the excess.

Now onto the mouth and nose. The nose should be small and look like a baby's snub nose. If the mouth or the teeth are too big, the figure appears dangerous. Place the mouth and nose halfway between the eyes. Create them with the Ellipse tool, Pathfinder panel and the Knife tool using the same techniques as before.

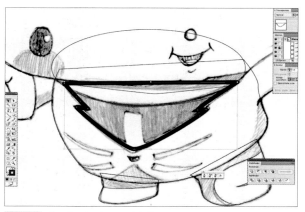

06 For the costume details, draw a dark shape with a 4pt weight using the Pen tool. Add an outline stroke (**Object > Path > Outline Stroke**). Remove its fill by changing its colour to [None], give it a 0.25pt black stroke, and delete the internal line. You should now have an empty element with just a line round it.

Draw a sloped rectangular shape and connect it to the other part of the costume details with your Pathfinder tools. Draw the other lines using the Pen tool. Ensure that everything fits to the volume of the body.

SIMPLE IS BEST

> Keep it simple! The reduction to the essentials emphasises the single elements. Children and adults likewise enjoy the little figures. Simple is cute! Besides, the characters become ageless.

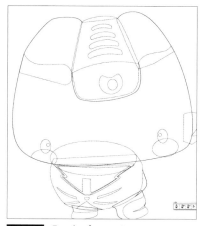

08 For the four stripes on our hero's forehead, first draw a 6pt curved line with rounded edges near the top of the central forehead element, then apply an Outline Stroke. Remove its fill, give it a 0.25pt black stroke, and delete the internal line.

Duplicate the shape, move it below and elongate it so that it has an appropriate size relative to the shape of the forehead. Repeat this procedure to create the other stripes.

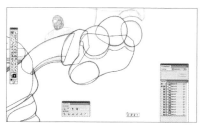

11 Draw short, round and fat arms with the Pen tool (again because of the baby-like proportions). Because of the enormous fingers relative to the hand and body, only create three fingers and a thumb in each hand. These should be blobby like a those of a chubby baby (as delicate skinny fingers like a newborn will look creepy).

Don't add too many details. Draw the palm of the hand with the Pen tool, and the fingers with the ellipse tool. Repeat the same procedures as before to create the areas that will be shaded.

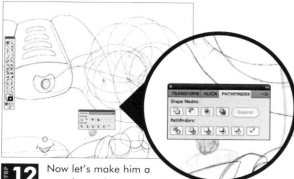

STEP 12 Now let's make him a superhero who can squirt a toxic cloud. Draw the rearmost part of the cloud with the Pen tool, then the cloud's head with the Ellipse tool. Unite them with the Pathfinder panel, copy them and then paste them in the back (**Cmd/Ctrl + C** then **Cmd/Ctrl + B**). Give the left shape of the head an outline of 1pt. Use the Knife tool to cut out 'stars' as shown.

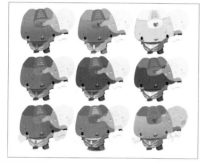

STEP 13 To find the best combination of colour, try out some variations. The cuteness of your character can be emphasised with colour.

While high contrast colours such as red and blue are powerful and used for adult superheroes like Superman, soft colours like pink, yellow and light blue are innocent and pure – and are perfect for cute figures. Because of their tonal value, pastel colours are also useful.

However, that doesn't mean that everything has to be pink – especially if you're aiming to appeal to a more mature audience. Also, too much white takes some energy out of the picture.

> To make your character look friendlier, choose a violet colour (C75, M100, Y0 and K0) instead of black for the eyes and the mouth.

STEP 14 The main part of the illustration is magenta, as this creates no huge and uneasy contrasts. Ensure that you avoid high contrasts when colouring the other shapes. Now the elements fit to the other colours much the better.

COLOUR ME BAD

> Dispense the colours in a not too precise way, then remove the black outlines. Now you can see where gradients and shades are missing and where colours do not distinguish from each other. Working without outlines offers a picturesque touch and allows more depth to be added to your shapes.

STEP 15 It's just a matter of tidying up and overall softening now – nothing in our artwork should have sharp edges. Give the main character's face lifework a white 2pt stroke with a rounded cap and corners.

Soften the curl of the cloud with the Convert Anchor Point tool (**Shift + C**). Apply a soft gradient to the main character's head. Apply some shadows below the head and the front of the cape by copying, pasting behind and changing this new element's colour to black. Give it a Multiply blending mode with an opacity of 60%, then apply a Gaussian Blur of 5 pixels (**Effect > Blur > Gaussian Blur**).

STEP 16 We need to integrate the figure into the background. The colour of the environment is bright in order to make the overall picture appear soft – but by using blue shades, the purple central character stands out. Strong colour contrasts have been avoided in the background and secondary characters. To maintain our overall tone, ensure you also use childlike characteristics when creating the fleeing figures. ■

PROFILE BUBBLEFRIENDS

> Bubblefriends, that is Sascha Preuß. He loves creating colorful vector illustrations. Bubblefriends have fun enriching the world with always-happy figures and pictures. In doing so, Sascha does not stop at illustration, toy or game design. Happy, cute and colourful are catchwords that are inseparably connected to the works of Bubblefriends. Vector is his main stylistic form, but trips into the world of painting and sculpture also define Bubblefriends.

CONTACT
• bubblefriends.de

Above top "One of my favourite characters. Created for a Bubblefriends exhibition last year," says Sascha.
Above Illustration for The Pixar Times website. "It was very funny to see my characters celebrating in a big party with the *Toy Story* guys," Sascha admits.

01 Open a new file in Flash. In the Properties window (**Cmd/Ctrl + F3**), click the Edit button and set the size to 420 x 594mm. Now import the base tracing file from the project files (*ht_trace.jpg*) by selecting **File > Import > Import to Stage (Cmd/Ctrl + R)**, and select the imported image. In the Align window (**Window > Align > To Stage**), select Align Horizontal Center and Align Vertical Center.

02 For detailed drawings, layering is vital. Flash manages layers in the Timeline window: rename and lock the tracing layer, then create a new layer for each element. Drawing in Flash is easy: using the Line tool (**N**), click and drag to create a straight line; click on the line and drag it to make a curve. Use the Line tool or Pen tool to trace all the elements apart from the focal lines.

03 Now let's create the focal lines. Use the Line tool to create a short vertical line at the point all the lines point to. Lock this layer and, in a new layer, draw black lines that drag out from the red focal point. Select all the lines, increase their line size to 8pt, and erase parts of the lines to make their length irregular. Select **Modify > Shape > Convert Lines to Fills**. Drag the edge point of each line to make them narrower at one end.

> **LEARN** BLACK AND WHITE ART

Monochrome
art in Flash

Keep things clear with black and white artwork, with Paul Shih

On this tutorial, character art guru Paul Shih shows how to create a detailed black-and-white artwork – using Flash. Shih says: "I personally find Flash's drawing system work best for the style we are making. It's fun and easy."

You'll learn handy tips for drawing in Flash, focusing on some essential drawing tools that make creating this artwork quick and simple. Starting with Flash's unique Line tools, we take this tool a step further by converting lines to create fills for a comic book-style 'focus lines' effect.

You'll also pick up tricks on maintaining visual clarity in a detailed black-and-white artwork. Feel free to embellish and add your own twists to the artwork as you create.

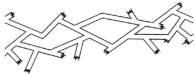

04 Now you've traced all the elements, they're ready to ink up – this is essentially colouring-in. Choose the colour – in this case we're only using black and white. Use the Paint Bucket tool (**B**) and click on the closed areas you've traced to fill with the paint.

05 To make elements stand out more and to separate them from their surroundings, thicken the outline of all elements, select an element, copy (**Cmd/Ctrl + C**), and create a new layer underneath, Paste the element in place (**Cmd/Ctrl + Shift + V**), increase the line size to your preference – I use 12pt for bear characters, and 15pt for the monster on top.

06 The artwork should be all inked up now – but you might feel that the colouring isn't quite perfect yet. Let's invert it. Select **File > Export > Export to Image**, and name it *invert.ai*. Open this file in Photoshop, and select **Image > Adjustments > Invert**. This trick is particularly useful for black-and-white images: you may find some parts work better this way than in the original, so adapt your Flash image accordingly.

07 Look for empty spaces – be creative, add some new elements to balance the positive and negative spaces. To create the metal pipes in middle, use the Line tool (**N**) to create some random pipe lines and increase the line size to 17pt. Convert the lines to fill, use the Ink Bottle tool (**S**) and click on the fills: this creates lines around the fill. You may want to import the PANDARA logo to your composition – it's in the project files (*pandara.eps*).

08 Finish up by adding some textures – 8-bit video games are good source of inspiration for this art style. Materials rendering is usually flat and simple, yet it symbolises materials so well. Once this is all done, it's a good idea to repeat the Photoshop Invert trick, play around, adjust it to your preference – and you'll have a unique *Hollow Threat* artwork. ∎

INFO PAUL SHIH

> New Zealand-based artist and designer Paul Shih is originally from Taiwan. His work is about events and characters, and is inspired by his surroundings. He says that this artwork, *Hollow Threat*, takes him back to his original love of drawing and doodling.

TIME TO COMPLETE
• 8-10 hours

SOFTWARE
• Adobe Flash, Photoshop

TIME TO COMPLETE
• 8-10 hours

PROJECT FILES
• Files for this tutorial are downloadable from *theartistsguide.co.uk/ downloads*

LouLou Tummie

> INFO

TIME TO COMPLETE
• 5 hours

SOFTWARE
• Adobe Illustrator

Design symmetrical character art

LouLou & Tummie create perfectly balanced characters

The beauty of this image lies in its simplicity: it's so clean and neatly proportioned that it radiates effortless charm. One key reason for its clear-cut appeal is its symmetry – by its very nature it's balanced and orderly, but it retains a sense of movement. It's also got a sort of comical formality, partly because its symmetry and background make it look almost like a heraldic crest.

In this tutorial, creative duo LouLou & Tummie show you how to use Illustrator to create a symmetrical, character-filled banner. You'll hone your use of the Pathfinder tool to build new shapes, and tweak lines to give them a sense of flow.

The tricks you'll learn are useful in a range of other vector-based illustrations, helping you to create art that is clean but not stilted.

To start, you'll need to get some reference images of plants and flowers and draw yourself a rough sketch to base the tutorial on.

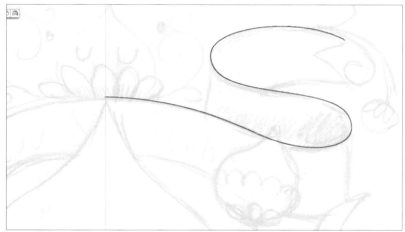

01 Import your sketch into a new Illustrator document, and set the opacity to 30%. Place a guideline in the middle of your artboard and align your image so that its centre is on the guideline. This guideline will be the pivotal element of your whole illustration. Use the Pen tool to trace the upper part of the banner on the right-hand side.

02 Hold down **Shift + Alt/Opt** and drag the line to copy it. This will be the bottom line of the banner. Select the endpoints and join them (**Cmd/Ctrl + J**). Close the two 'open' sides of the banner by drawing two shapes over it. Make sure nothing sticks out of the banner. Select all (**Cmd/Ctrl + A**) and go **Window > Pathfinder > Divide**, then ungroup.

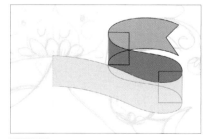

03 The banner is now composed of three parts: top, middle and bottom. Select the pieces that belong to the bottom part and choose Add to Shape in Pathfinder. Click Expand. Repeat for the two other parts. Select all and click on the Reflect tool then, while holding **Alt/Opt**, click on the guide in the middle. Choose **Vertical > Copy**.

04 Draw the right–hand side of your central flower or figure, making sure you start on the guideline. Drag as you place the second anchor point, so that you can make smooth, flowing lines that you can then adjust later.

It's best to place as few anchor points on a curve as you can – this makes it flow better. Reflect the line vertically on the guideline (as in Step 3). Select and join the endpoints.

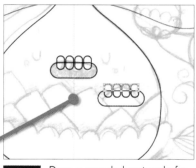

> **Make sure everything is centred at all times.**

05 Drag a rounded rectangle for the mouth and a smaller one for the teeth. Drag and copy the 'tooth' (**Shift + Alt/Opt**), then **Cmd/Ctrl + D** to repeat this. Copy the mouth and teeth, choose Divide in the Pathfinder tool and ungroup. Delete the parts you don't need and place the teeth back in the mouth.

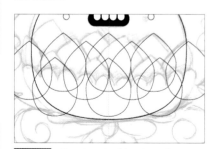

06 Create a leaf by dragging a circle, then using the Convert Anchor Point tool (**Shift + C**) and clicking on the top anchor point of the circle. Select this anchor point and nudge it up a little to give the leaf a point, making it a teardrop shape. Place the leaf according to your sketch and make multiple copies. Adjust the outer leaves so that they fit your sketch. ❯

07 Drag a small circle. Select it and grab it by the left anchor point. Hold **Shift + Alt/Opt** and move the circle to the right until it snaps to the furthest right anchor point and release. Use the **Cmd/Ctrl + D** to copy this action. Draw a curve and reflect it to create the bottom part of the flower, then join the endpoints. Select all the circles and the bottom shape and then select **Pathfinder > Add to Shape > Expand**.

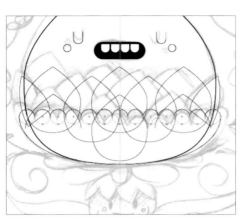

> **>** Creating organic shapes is much easier with a graphics tablet.

08 Now let's draw the swirly vines. Again, we draw only the left (or right) side of the illustration and then reflect it. Try to draw lines by hand using the Pencil tool as this gives a more spontaneous feel to your image. They don't have to be perfect, but try to limit the amount of adjusting they need.

09 Next, clean up the points you don't need from the lines – use Delete Anchor Point (-) from the Pen menu. Fewer anchor points means a better flow. Drag the curve handles on the anchor points (use the white arrow) and tweak them until the lines have the right flow. This will take some time and practice.

> "Try to draw lines by hand using the pencil tool as this gives a more spontaneous feel to your image"

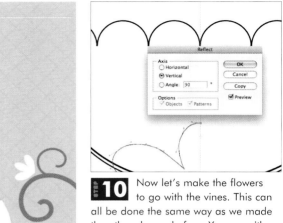

10 Now let's make the flowers to go with the vines. This can all be done the same way as we made the other shapes before. You can either copy the central figure, resize it and add some new detail, or you can play around with new shapes if you prefer.

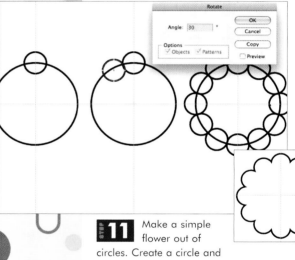

11 Make a simple flower out of circles. Create a circle and drag a guide from the top and side to the middle of the circle. Centre a small circle on the top anchor point of the bigger one. Tap **R** and **Alt/Opt + click** in the middle of the big circle, then rotate it 30°. Repeat this (**Cmd/Ctrl + D**) until you have enough circles. Select all and in the Pathfinder palette select **Add to Shape > Expand**.

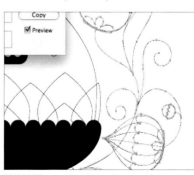

12 Finish all the flowers, leaves and curls on one side of the illustration. When you feel this side looks good, select all the flowers, curls and vines and use the Reflect tool to copy and flip it.

STEP 13 Now for the faces. Create a mouth, as in Step 5. Draw the eye, the freckles and cheek on the left side and then reflect them to the right. Again, use a guide in the middle to keep the face symmetrical – this is a great timesaver. Group the face (**Cmd/Ctrl + G**) and place it on the flower. Rotate it (**R**) to fit.

STEP 14 You will need to add some details to finish the illustration. Placing these randomly, rather than perfectly symmetrically, will liven up your illustration. These could be little leaves, dots, scales, extra curls – whatever you fancy.

STEP 15 Now adjust the line weight to get it just right. Also, check that your shapes are fully closed by making them black – if the lines aren't properly connected then the black will fill the artboard. You may need to reorder some of the shapes, moving them to the front or back.

Two examples of LouLou & Tummie's colourful, vibrant character art with *Anatomy Bot* (**top**) and *Flowerpot* (**below**).

STEP 16 When you're happy with the illustration in black-and-white you can start colouring. Some people prefer to colour as they go along, but you can often get a better feel for the lines and shapes when they're black and white. Colouring is also much faster when your composition is already finished.

INFO

TIME TO COMPLETE
• 2-3 hours

SOFTWARE
• Adobe Illustrator CS4 or higher,
Photoshop CS4 or higher

PROJECT FILES
• Files for this tutorial
can be downloaded from
*theartistsguide.co.uk/
downloads*

Create cartoon figures with ease

Mercedes Crespo shows how you can swiftly draw an appealing character based on a few simple shapes

On this tutorial, Mercedes Crespo (aka YemaYema) shows how she creates her appealing cartoon characters. Though full of detail, rich in colour and complex in appearance, they are simple to draw, as she reveals here.

With just the Pencil tool plus basic shapes and a good eye for colour and composition, you can make your illustrations go a long way. Mercedes stresses the importance of having fun and playing around with shapes. It is possible to achieve great things when you least expect it and exploring is a good way of allowing this to happen.

In our project files, you'll find Mercedes' original sketch and a texture file you'll use to add depth to your composition.

03 Start adding the simplest details to the character – two circles will do for eyes, while for the mouth, create a circle and split it. Now select the Pen tool and click on both ends to close it up.

04 Hide the background layer where the sketch is. Now let's focus on the torso. Grab the Pen tool and create a shape for the shirt. Just trace the outer corners of the jacket to create the inner white shape. Adjust with the Direct Selection tool; you need to have precise and clean lines. Work with the neck of the coat as you need to.

05 Now we are going to add more detail using the same technique I used to create the white shirt. To give the coat an 'inner outline', use the Pen tool and a darker colour. For the cheeks, create a circle in a contrasting colour and then another circle inside that in an even richer hue. ❯

01 First I start with a quick sketch (available from the Download Zone), containing basic shapes that will determine the composition and how the character will look. I try to leave it open for revision, and it isn't meant to look finished. It's just something done quickly to get an idea down.

02 In Illustrator, select **File > Place**, bring the sketch into what will be a background layer and lock it. Create a new layer where you will create basic shapes that trace out the image, for example just a circle for the head, a rectangle for the shorts. Remember to play with the composition and change things if you need to.

> "I start with a quick sketch, just something done quickly to get an idea down"

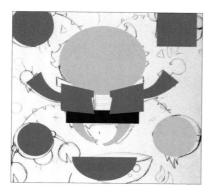

06 Now we are going to start fleshing out our little pirate. For the hair, just draw a swirly shape. Add more detail to the eyes by creating more circles that act as white reflections. For the teeth, simply create rectangles. Incidentally, I freehand a lot so I also make sure to remove surplus anchor points using the Pen tool.

09 Create eyelashes by adding small triangles around the eye, which will also serve as shading. Connect the minor characters to our pirate using arcs (create a circle, delete the colour inside and then delete one of the four anchor points).

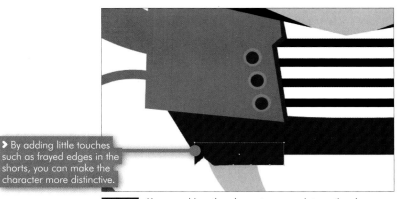

> By adding little touches such as frayed edges in the shorts, you can make the character more distinctive.

10 Keep making the character more interesting by adding a bit more detail. To finish the trousers, create a rectangle and then select the Pen tool and add anchor points to the base of the rectangle. Then move every other anchor point here upwards to create the ripped effect.

07 To add more detail to the hair, you can create more locks and strands with the Pencil tool. Be creative and once again, remember to remove surplus anchor points. For the nose, let's use simple triangles.

08 To create the character's hook, draw a rectangle for the base and make it taper. Then add an ellipse to give a bit of shading and depth. To fit it flush against the sleeve, just group the objects that make the hook's base (hold **Shift** and select, then **right click > Group**) and move them together.

11 To create the water, select the Pencil tool and freehand big drops of water, then add some detail to them. Let's give our pirate some highlights on the trousers and coat, too, by adding zigzag shapes in a colour that stands out. Also finish the nose by creating more triangles.

12 Now it's time to add clouds and other decorations. Copy and Paste and place where desired, paying attention to the composition. Make it fun – experiment, play with shapes and let your creativity guide you.

13 Happy with your design? If so, that's as far as we're going to go in Illustrator. Now we'll import the file into Photoshop to add texture.

14 In Photoshop, open *texture layer.psd* from the Download Zone. Select All, then Copy and Paste it into your design. Set the blending mode to Screen and the opacity to 23. Adjust until you're satisfied.

15 Select the Burn tool and paint over the edges to give it some shadow. In the Options bar, set the Range drop-down menu to Midtones and add some shade to corners. Think about basic shading when doing this.

16 Finally, select the Dodge tool. Set the Range drop-down menu to Highlights and add highlights in the eyes, cheeks, and certain corners to make them pop out a bit more. ■

PROFILE YEMAYEMA

> Mercedes Crespo, better known as YemaYema, was born in Guayaquil, Ecuador. Now 27, she has been drawing since she was 15, though she wasn't sure of her artistic direction until a few years ago, when she discovered a book from the Berlin-based Pictoplasma Project. Since then, she has loved drawing even more and continues to develop her own style, hoping it evolves into something even more distinctive. T-shirts and other items bearing her artwork can be bought from her website.

CONTACT
• *yemayema.com*

The image immediately above was Mercedes' entry for Outsmart 2010, a project to create artwork featuring Smart cars. The other two images are her designs for T-shirts made by emptees (*emptees.com*).

To **Haiti** with love

Learn how 12 artists from the **Blood Sweat Vector** collective came together to design art in aid of earthquake victims

O t's essential to be able to work in teams, so we're often told, but how do you do it well when your collaborators are scattered across the globe? The Renmen Project (*therenmenproject.co.uk*) makes a heartwarming case study. It was set up by Ben The Illustrator and design blog collective Thunder Chunky following the earthquake that devastated Haiti in January 2010. Their fundraising project continues to roll a year on, with the release of a series of type-art prints benefiting Unicef's Haiti appeal.

Thunder Chunky's Stephen Chan is also a member of the international Blood Sweat Vector collective. After discussions with BSV's Jared Nickerson (aka J3Concepts) and Kate McInnes (loungekat), they came up with the idea of doing artistic prints of the letters in 'Renmen' – the Haitian word for 'love' – with two artists jointly creating each letter. "We thought it would allow flexibility in the collaborations between each pair," says Stephen, "and it would strengthen the message behind Renmen."

The pairings fell into place quite naturally. "Out of common sense, some geographic positioning and timing, we all gathered to create the most awesome collaborative project ever," says Stephen, modestly.

Being fans of each other's work brought Chris Leavens and Alexandra Zutto (aka Zutto) together for the letter R (*above right*). Geographical proximity helped Australians Travis Price and Okayboss create the second N, while in France Guillaume Pain (Tougui) and Hosmane Benahmed (IKS) hatched the second E.

As for the first E, Kate bent the rules a tad by working on it with Sean Kelly, her partner in the illustration duo McKelly – and not a BSV member. Jared and Ruben Cantuni (aka TokyoCandies), who devised the first N, were already good friends. Finally, Stephen partnered up with Junichi Tsuneoka (aka Stubborn Sideburn) in what he calls a "superhuman Asian illustration entity" to do the M.

Engaging 12 illustrators with wildly contrasting styles could have resulted in a disconnected set of artworks, but Stephen wanted harmony. He wrote a simple brief explaining the positive messages that The Renmen Project wanted to evoke. He also sent round a template to provide guidance on the letters' dimensions and shape, plus a primary and secondary colour swatch.

Of the letter he co-designed, Stephen says: "I wanted it to happen organically, to inspire and excite," he says. "I explained my intentions, adding some illustrations to the letter template and passing it on [to Junichi]. We discussed our ideas each time the piece was exchanged, so that it grew the way we both wanted it to. Our angled, character-driven styles slotted together naturally, and we ended up with a creation that we're both very proud of."

This tutorial gives a glimpse of that collaborative process through the work of Chris and Zutto. They bounced an Illustrator file between their respective homes in California and Miass, Russia, until they felt their letter was complete.

Stephen feels the project was a way for him to use his skills to make a difference. "This is why I really like being an illustrator," he says. "Illustrators are truly the nicest people, and without their help none of this could have happened. Hopefully we can sell everything and donate 100 per cent of the proceeds to Haiti."

> "Illustrators are truly the nicest people, and without their help none of this could have happened"

Stephens awesome cover for the new Publishers Club magazine *Totummy*.

PROFILE STEPHEN CHAN

> Based in Liverpool, Stephen describes his design style this way: "It's character-driven and often involves isometric detailed landscapes and scenes. I try to implement as much detail and make the illustration as fun as possible."

CONTACT
• *stephen-chan.co.uk*

> **INFO**

TIME TO COMPLETE
• "That's a bit of a mystery as we put this together over the course of months," says Chris.

SOFTWARE
• Adobe Illustrator

01 Zutto kicked off the collaboration with Chris by doing a preparatory sketch of the R. Her aim was to remix the most fun ideas, characters and landscape elements from her sketchbooks into one piece. Her main inspiration was that 'renmen' means 'love' in Haitian Creole.

That initial sketch turned out to be the most complicated part of the project for Zutto, because she constantly had to bear in mind how the ingredients she was introducing might best fit in with Chris's style.

02 Upon receiving the sketch, Chris felt it was "filled with lovely Zutto creatures and landscape elements". He began vectoring in his contribution, intertwining his characters with hers. "I loved that she chose an outdoor scenario because most of my artwork is heavily nature-inspired," he says. ▶

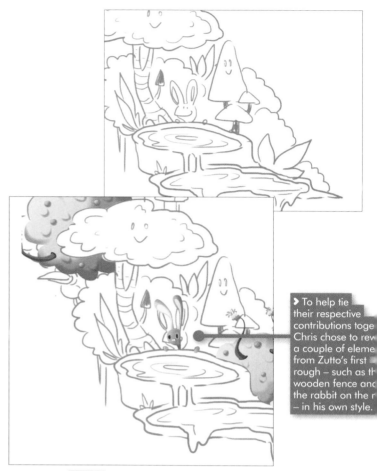

> To help tie their respective contributions toge Chris chose to rew a couple of eleme from Zutto's first rough – such as th wooden fence and the rabbit on the r – in his own style.

04 Chris added in more elements, keeping the forms flat and simple. "That's my approach to vector art – start with basic forms and add in the details later," he says.

03 When Zutto received that first coloured version from Chris, containing his creatures and landscape elements, it gave her a lot of ideas on how she might develop the work. First, though, she wanted to get the broad strokes of colour down. "I filled all of the large shapes, such as trees, rocks, hills, clouds and main characters, to get a vision of whole composition in colour," she says. "Then I sent the result back to Chris."

05 The next step for Zutto was to start smoothing out the differences between her and Chris' styles, and to add some more details.

"I started from the bottom-right rock with two lakes," she says. "I spent much time choosing different colour combinations for all my large elements. The colours of the big shapes are really important for overall look."

Above *Forest Friends* – "Never know what can be inside your pockets", Zutto says cryptically.

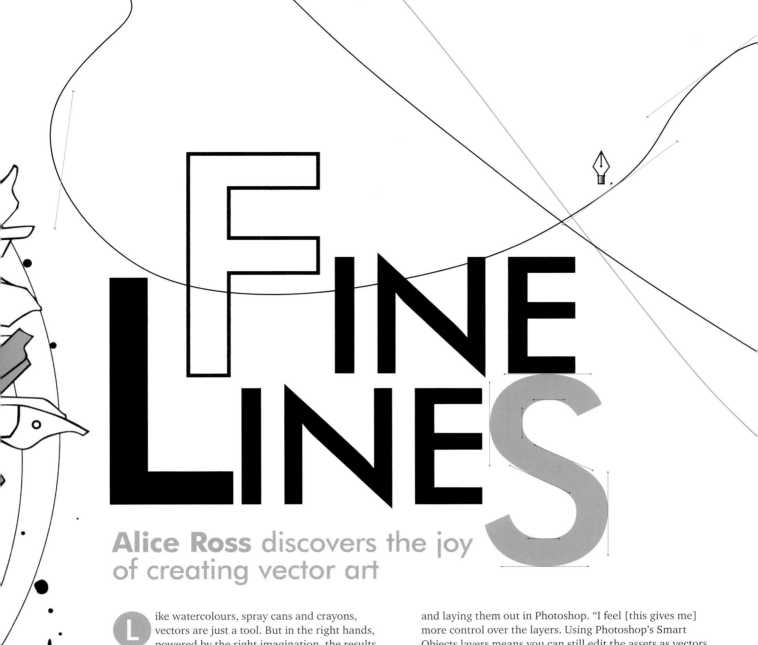

FINE LINES

Alice Ross discovers the joy of creating vector art

Like watercolours, spray cans and crayons, vectors are just a tool. But in the right hands, powered by the right imagination, the results of vector-based graphics can be spectacular.

There are certain areas where vectors really seem to take flight. For character art, the ability to render figures in a couple of shapes is hugely attractive.

"I think there is something appealing about the simple, geometric shapes that vector-based characters are made out of," says Jon Ball of illustration and graphic design firm Pokedstudio (see page 108). "Also, [character designers like] the clean lines and fills that are a feature of much vector work."

The combination of the digital crispness of vectors with raw, natural scenes – as shown by Adrian Van Delzel on page 106 – makes a gorgeous counterpoint, which hints at a sharper version of nature hiding inside your computer, like a 21st-century Narnia. Of his style of work, Adrian says: "I needed a medium that enables me to give expression and inspiration to thousands of details; the light forms and lines [of vector art] seemed very attractive for this."

Others, such as Magnus Blomster (see page 107), prefer a less obviously digital look, painstakingly recreating a hand-drawn style, Vector art has its pitfalls, though.

"Vectors can be very hard to work with in terms of layers and file size if you're working at 300dpi," explains Jon, "and it can get very fiddly grouping and selecting stuff within groups. Start adding in effects and the file soon starts to lag." He gets around this problem by taking vectors and laying them out in Photoshop. "I feel [this gives me] more control over the layers. Using Photoshop's Smart Objects layers means you can still edit the assets as vectors if needed," Jon explains.

Another issue with vector-based work is that Illustrator can seem so simple to use, it's easy to get caught up in the whizzy features and forget about the artistic basics.

"There is a lot of samey work out there," says Magnus. "I guess people find it easy to trace photographs without adding any sort of personal touch to it."

Adrian believes that just because Illustrator puts the rainbow at your fingertips, it doesn't mean you have to make use of the whole spectrum. He bemoans "the strange use of colours – often you come across very good compositions, very well thought-out, but they're ruined by their colour range."

Meanwhile, illustrator Gary Fernández (see page 109) argues that there's a more fundamental issue at hand, one that lies at the heart of the phrase 'digital art'. "I feel that digital is considered an end, rather than a means. In general, people tend to think about how to resolve an image in the least time possible, rather than thinking about how to obtain a better image. The result is an image that lacks soul and is crammed with effects."

Each of the artists we showcase here has gone beyond the boundaries of genre to create illustrations that, while they're made from vectors, are so much more than their means of creation. Perhaps the key is to master the tool – and only then, focus on the work.

Adrian Van Delzel
Animal magic

The enigmatic digital artworks of Barcelona-based artist Adrian Van Delzel are populated by strange creatures that only come out at night. Looking at his artwork is a little like spotting Bigfoot in *Fantasia* – the exotic beasts stand frozen and symmetrical in the middle of fantastically detailed psychedelic landscapes.

"My images always have a central theme, normally one that's related to nature and to hidden feelings," he explains. The mystery of his images is intentional: he describes them as an attempt to communicate complex feelings that are hard to express in words, as well as "tracings of melancholy and of our roots as animals."

Inspiration arrives in a complete form for Adrian. After sketching his creatures in pencil, "I never retouch or change them: they come out exactly as they are," he says. Adrian traces his scanned pencil sketches in Illustrator before digitally adding a landscape.

This apparent simplicity belies the immense detail that Adrian works in. "In many cases, the process takes me weeks," he says. "For example, [in *Secret Spirit*] each of those feathers is made up of four or five layers, overlaid with transparencies. I'm an obsessive."

Finally, he creates the lighting effects. "They're little more than Clipping Masks and gradients, overlaid on the final composition," he says.

Adrian has long been impressed by vector art. "I remember seeing the work of other [vector] artists and being left speechless – it seemed unattainable." Having taught himself Illustrator, it's become his key tool. "I don't use any other programs – it seems like a betrayal," he explains. "If I start with vectors, I finish with them."

Adrian finds that there's an inherent minimalism to working with Illustrator. "Vectors limit me to showing only what needs to be shown," he says. "Without them, my art wouldn't be the same."
adrianvandelzel.com

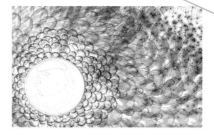

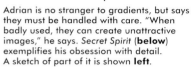

Adrian is no stranger to gradients, but says they must be handled with care. "When badly used, they can create unattractive images," he says. *Secret Spirit* (**below**) exemplifies his obsession with detail. A sketch of part of it is shown **left**.

⚲ **PRO** *VECTOR TIP*

"FOR THOSE WHO ARE STARTING OUT: BE PATIENT. FOR THOSE WHO HAVE ALREADY MASTERED VECTORS: EXPERIMENT... A LOT. FOR THOSE WHO WANT TO START: BE AWARE THAT IT'S VERY TIME-CONSUMING."

– Adrian Van Delzel

Magnus Blomster
The ladies' man

A cover (**right**) for record label Ad Noiseam, who Magnus describes as one of his favourite clients.

Not all artists want their work to instantly seem digital. Magnus Blomster combines Illustrator with a hand-drawn style to make the image seem an implausibly perfect pen-and-ink drawing.

"My main reason for choosing vectors is that I am a perfectionist," he says. "If something goes wrong – no matter how insignificant – when I'm doing an ink drawing, I start over from scratch and thus very rarely finish any. I don't think it aids my style in any particular way since my style is what it is – but it has certainly increased the rate of finished images."

Magnus' often erotic images feature women surrounded by curlicues. He describes his style as a blend of Art Nouveau ("I have known and loved [it] since I was a little boy," he says) with religious symbolism, pornography and "general weirdness".

His work refuses to fit into illustration trends – possibly because he never set out to be a professional illustrator. "I've always drawn. The

getting paid for doing it part just sort of happened by itself."

To create a piece, Magnus scans a pencil sketch, then painstakingly traces its lines as closed paths. "I always use the Pen tool with 0.1pt red lines on top of a sketch, to be able to see what I'm doing," he explains.

He selects everything on the layer, removes the lines and, in a separate layer, fills the shapes. "After that, still with everything selected, I bring up the Pathfinder and use the Unite tool, then hit Expand to make everything on the layer one single shape."

Finally, he adds layers for the background and face colours. He uses the Pen, Ellipse and Pathfinder tools – "No other effect or filters or trickery. All lines are filled shapes."

The secret of Magnus' success is to work in immense detail while avoiding fancy tools. This approach keeps file sizes manageable, but it's also key to the way he views Illustrator: "more as a pen than a program," he says.
blomster.tumblr.com ❯

✒ **PRO** *VECTOR TIP*

"DON'T TREAT ILLUSTRATOR AS SOMETHING THAT'S GOING TO MAKE THE IMAGES FOR YOU"
– Magnus Blomster

For this personal work (sketch and rough **above**, final piece **right**), Magnus was aiming to create something less complicated than his usual style.

Pokedstudio
The right character

"I love to create slightly offbeat characters and weird worlds," says Jon Ball. In his professional guise as Pokedstudio, he has turned this love into a career, creating quirky yet highly polished miniature worlds for clients including MTV, the BBC, PlayStation, Doritos and Penguin Books.

Jon explains that vectors are a natural fit for the way he works – "I like using simple geometric shapes to create characters and worlds" – but it's not the only application he'll use. "I do about half my work in vectors, and half using 3D; most pieces tend to be a mix. I usually take works into Photoshop for some final editing," he adds.

To illustrate his creative process, Jon talked us through how he created his art print *Octobeast*. He says: "I started with a sketch – though I don't always. Often my sketches are very simple, just the main element and its relationship to the rest of the picture. I then create some simple shapes in Illustrator. The most complex shape in this picture was probably the eye."

He continues: "I used various gradient fills for the iris and for the lens. Using custom brushes I created some veins around the eyeball, and made some transparent layers for highlights."

Other elements were brought in on separate layers, then he exported the image into Photoshop to add in the creased-paper texture. "This could be done in Illustrator, but it starts to get really slow when you add large raster layers in," Jon says.

While the methods involved in creating images like this are surprisingly simple, Jon points out that the skills needed are anything but. "You could argue that these vector characters are simple to make and less time-consuming than a hand-drawn or 3D character, but having experience in most media I don't think that's true. You need a certain eye to get the proportions and shapes of vector characters right. Creating good and unique characters in Illustrator is just as hard as in any other media."

pokedstudio.com

There's no shortage of Pokedstudio's trademark "offbeat characters and weird worlds" in *Morning of Doom* (**top**), *Deadly Dog* (**above**) and *Octobeast* (**below**).

✒ **PRO** *VECTOR TIP*

"Most successful art is liked because of the meaning behind an image. So make art that has some reason to exist"
– Jon Ball

Gary Fernández
Mr Clean

↑ **PRO** VECTOR TIP

"FIND YOUR OWN WAY OF USING THE TOOLS, TO ACHIEVE SOMETHING THAT'S TRULY YOUR OWN"

– Gary Fernández

Stylised and elegant, with a muted – almost sombre – colour palette, Gary Fernández's images are digital art at its sharpest. The Spaniard moved from graphic design in fashion magazines into illustration, providing imagery for high-profile ad campaigns and showing his work in exhibitions worldwide.

This sharpness is what draws him to vectors. "I like the cleanness of line," he says. His figures are often set against blank backdrops, but they're usually surrounded by very detailed elements.

Vectors have another advantage. "I like the ability to work on details to the maximum [size], which is only possible with vectors," he says.

The same principle works at the other end of the scale: vectors can be scaled infinitely. For artists like Gary, whose illustrations sometimes appear on billboards, that's a big relief.

This method also makes it easy to experiment, allowing Gary to play with colours and placement of elements. However, as with all the artists we spoke to, his creativity doesn't begin on a screen.

"My first stage is with pencil and paper," he explains. "Then I work up each of the elements until I achieve a detail and a form that I like.

"Then comes the vector stage, which is when I trace all the drawings, develop the composition and the details," he says, explaining that he works on each element individually before arranging them in the final composition. Next he adds colour, limiting his palette to the bare minimum.

"The final stage is Photoshop, where I polish imperfection and give the final touches," he says.

It's a simple but detailed process – in terms of Illustrator tools Gary uses little more than "Knife, Scissors, Eraser and above all Cmd + Z." His results are slick but what shines through most is the imagination, hovering in a circus-like space somewhere between Disney and Dalí.

garyfernandez.net

Below, far right
A series of festive images Gary produced last year for the Globus department store in Switzerland.
Right Gary usually starts his work with a pencil sketch.

> **INFO**

TIME TO COMPLETE
• 45 minutes

SOFTWARE
• Adobe Illustrator CS5

PROJECT FILES
• Files for this tutorial
are downloadable from
*theartistsguide.co.uk/
downloads*

Faux 3D finishes in Illustrator

Create vibrant 3D illustrations using a few simple effects

K aran Singh shows you a clever and ridiculously quick way of giving your flat illustrations a faux 3D finish – without leaving the confines of Illustrator.

Karan finds Photoshop's 3D lighting tools to be cumbersome, and says that Illustrator is more than capable of creating depth and dimension, using such effects as the inner and outer glows and the Gaussian blur.

Here, he focuses on one element of the artwork, but the techniques were used throughout.

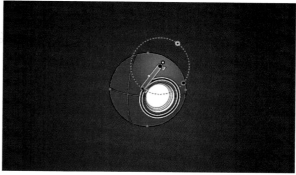

01 First off, grab the greyscale droid (*TUTDROID.AI*) I've created from the project files, and open it up in Illustrator. You're more than welcome to create your own object and use this tutorial as a guide to colouring and lighting. The beauty of this technique is that it's applicable to almost any shape.

02 We're going to use a set of gradient swatches to colour the shape. For this tutorial, I've already created a set of rich blue swatches, which you will find on the 'Palette' layer of *TUT-DROID.AI*.

If blue isn't your thing – or you're using your own image for this tutorial – create dark, mid and light versions of your chosen hue.

03 What I've found crucial in helping define how to colour a shape is the creation of a light source. Setting this up is as simple as drawing a circle on the canvas to distinguish where the light is coming from.

A guide like this comes in handy when your illustration becomes more complex and confusing as you lose count of the shapes and gradients used.

Create this object on a separate layer and lock it.

04 Let's go back to the shape. Using the light source as a reference, begin colouring the droid. Start with the base as this helps define how the others are coloured.

Using the Gradient tool (**G**) with the Shape option selected, click and drag on the shape to define the gradation of the gradient. I've used the lightest gradient for the base and set it to 'Radial' in the Gradient palette (**Window > Gradient**).

Ensure that the lighter shade of the gradient corresponds to the position of the light source. In this case, the lighter colour in the gradient begins at the top as the light source is above the droid.

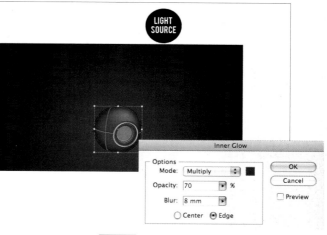

05 The second step to adding depth to the shape is giving the base of the droid an inner glow. An inner glow is useful as, regardless of the angles of the gradient, it creates a shadow that follows the edge of the shape, giving it a bevelled appearance.

With the base shape of the droid selected, chose **Effects > Stylize > Inner Glow**. Select the 'Edge' option, a shadow colour and a blur amount. If you're using my droid and colour scheme, select #123860 as the colour with a Blur of 8mm.

Choose Multiply for the blending mode. Set the opacity to 70% for a rich, dark shadow. As shapes vary, so does the level of blur applied; the smaller the shape, the less the amount of blur. ▶

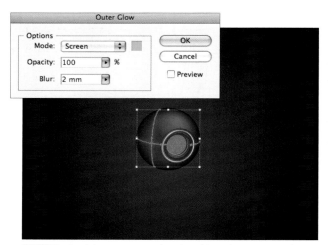

STEP 06

Applying an outer glow is achieved using a similar process to the previous stage, except it obviously occurs outside of the shape, using Outer Glow.

Personally, I like to use this tool sparingly as it allows you to accentuate certain features of an object, without looking like everything's glowing. For example, here I want to give the impression that the pink elements in the droid are glowing.

To do this, select the shape, then choose **Effects > Stylize > Outer Glow**. As with the Inner Glow options, adjust the blending mode, blur and opacity. Leave the blending mode as Screen, as this is ideal for objects on darker backgrounds, with 100% opacity for maximum glow and a 2mm Blur. I used a light pink for the glow colour (#FF92BC).

STEP 07

The next few steps are pivotal in creating the final effects. We're going to create a custom brush that tapers, widens and then tapers again. This brush is going to be used for highlights and shadows

Create a new layer. Select the Arc tool, which is on the Toolbar under the Line Segment tool. When selected, hold **Shift** while you drag the tool across to create an equally proportional arc.

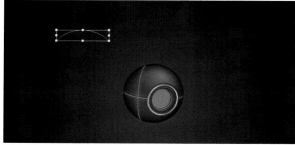

STEP 08

Select your newly created arc and rotate it 45° clockwise (**Object > Transform > Rotate -45°**), until it's horizontal with the ends facing down. You should now be seeing half of your tapered brush stroke.

We need to mirror this line, in order to make a shape out of it. To do this, first **right-click** and select **Transform > Reset Bounding Box**.

STEP 09

Select the line and hold **Alt**, whilst dragging it to create a duplicate. With the duplicate selected, choose **Object > Transform > Rotate** and set the value to 180°. Click OK, and your result should be a mirrored version of the arc.

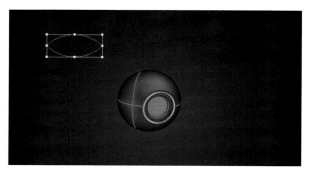

STEP 10

For the next step, switch on Smart Guides (**Cmd/Ctrl + U**), and move the duplicated arc to match up with the ends of the original arc. The best way to do this in Selection tool mode (**V**) is by dragging the arc by either of its end anchor points, and lining it up to the corresponding end of the other arc.

After lining up the anchor points correctly, your cursor will change from black to white.

Select both the arcs, **right-click** and choose Join. This joins the anchor points. The two arcs are now a shape.

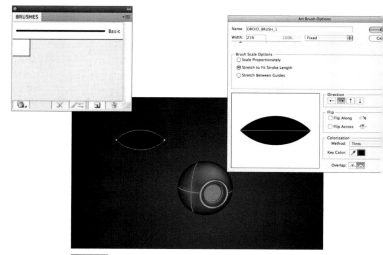

STEP 11

Select your new shape and fill it with black. Open the brush palette, if necessary (**Window > Brushes** or **F5**), and select New Brush (the button to the left of the trashcan). From the types that follow, choose Art Brush.

In the Art Brush Options dialog that opens, set the brush width to 25% and the Colourisation value to Tints. Hit OK.

We've finished making our highlights and shadows brush, so you can delete the merged arc shape from the canvas.

> "Use your newly created brush... The locations of the highlights and shadows are defined by the direction of your light source"

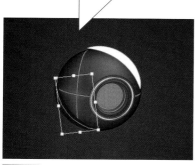

12 Create a new layer above the droid and call it 'Effects'. Use your newly created brush to create a 3-pixel highlight stroke in white (#FFFFFF) in the top left edge of the shape, then a 3-pixel shadow stroke in dark blue (#022E44) in the bottom-right edge of the shape.

The locations of the highlights and shadows are defined by the direction of your light source.

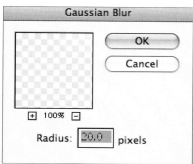

13 Blur the highlight and shadow strokes by selecting one stroke. From the top menu, choose **Effects > Blur > Gaussian Blur**.

As with the inner and outer glows, the blur radius is usually relative to the site of the object. In this case, I chose a 20-pixel radius. The larger the radius, the softer the colour. Repeat the same process for the shadow stroke.

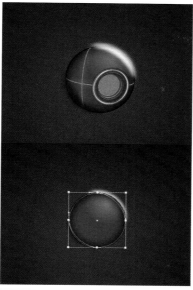

14 You'll notice that the blur is bleeding past the surface area of the droid. Our next step is to create a clipping mask to rectify this. Group the highlight and shadow strokes by selecting both of them, and then **Cmd/Ctrl + G**.

From the droid layer, select the base of the shape, copy it (**Cmd/Ctrl +C**) and paste it in place (**Cmd/Ctrl + F**) in the 'Effects' layer.

15 Now the droid's base should be on top of the blurred strokes. Select both the base of the droid you've just pasted and the grouped strokes, then **Object > Clipping Mask > Make** (or **Cmd/Ctrl + 7**). Strokes bleeding outside of the shape are now contained within the droid's outline.

16 Out of personal preference, I added some additional blurred shapes to the droid's pink eye. These were created in the same way as the strokes, but with filled-in shapes. ■

PROFILE KARAN SINGH

> Karan Singh is an freelance illustrator based in Melbourne, Australia. He's had over four years experience working in a studio and independently on projects, ranging from typography to apparel design to illustration.

When he's not illustrating he's writing for his self-initiated design blog, Pig Bimpin'. Drop him an email at *karan@wakeupmrsingh.com*

CONTACT
• *wakeupmrsingh.com*

Above top *K4000*, a self-initiated personal work for Depthcore's *Mirror* exhibition. It was inspired by retro futurism, Aldous Huxley's *Brave New World* and the work of Syd Mead
Above *R is for Replicant* Inspired by Ridley Scott's *Blade Runner*. It was created with Matei Apostolescu.

> **LEARN** DYNAMIC ILLUSTRATOR

Create lush, **glossy vector** images

Discover how Illustrator's Gaussian Blur can transform your art

Ot's easy to associate vectors with flat shapes – but creating Illustrator images with real depth needn't be a headache. In this tutorial, Thomas Burden (who works under the name ...There Will Be Unicorns) shows how you can create striking, vibrant work in Illustrator using a simple colour palette and basic blur effects – particularly Illustrator's built-in Gaussian Blur effects.

Along the way, you'll also learn how to bring simple shapes to life, and how to create charming characters and elements, using only basic Illustrator and Photoshop.

Shading elements in Illustrator with the Gaussian Blur leaves your objects completely editable. Once you've scaled these elements to the right size, you can import them into Photoshop for a quick brightening up and some tweaks to layer blending modes and styles.

The net effect is fresh, clean and irresistibly cheerful.

04 Select the red shape that I created from a basic rounded rectangle shape. This will form the base of the rainbow volcano, and, once shaded, coloured and duplicated, will form the rest of it too. Hit **Cmd/Ctrl + G** to group the object and double-click it to enter the group. Now draw a highlight line with the Pen tool (**P**), just inside the top left of the shape, with a white stroke and a thickness of 3.5 pixels with rounded ends.

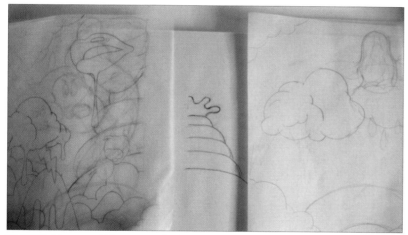

01 It's a good idea to start by sketching on paper: I find it easier and quicker to mark out rough compositions and characters or elements by hand first. These are very rough, though, and I don't even bother scanning them in, preferring to take snapshots with a digital camera for speed. Scan yours in if you prefer.

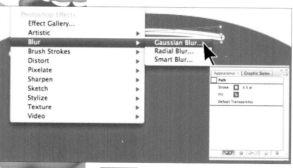

05 With line selected click **Effect > Blur > Gaussian Blur** and set it to 10. You will see the effect appear in the Appearances panel on the right. If this is not open then select **Window > Appearance** from the menu or use **Shift + F6**. Double-click the effect in the appearances panel at any time to edit it.

02 Loosely trace these jottings in Illustrator, using the basic Shape tools in combination with the Pen tool to keep a uniform and simple look to all the elements. Then choose a colour palette – keep this as simple as possible. I usually use no more than 10 colours. Use these as a base to work with while getting the major compositional elements in place.

03 We'll focus on creating one element, as almost everything is created using the same process. Open *Rainbow Volcano.ai* from the project files in Illustrator. Then select **Illustrator > Preferences > General**. Tick the box marked Scale Strokes & Effects. This ensures that any stroke and effect applied to an object will scale relatively to the object it is applied to – which is key here, as adding strokes and effects is the bulk of what we'll be doing.

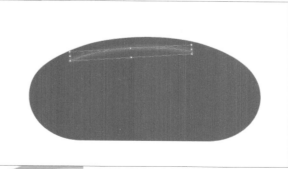

06 Now reduce the opacity of the line to 29%. There you have it – a highlight. ➤

07 Now we need to mask the group so that any shading we apply stays within the borders of the shape. Select the background shape again and go **Cmd/Ctrl + C > Cmd/Ctrl + F > Cmd/Ctrl + Shift +]** to copy it and paste in the same place, then bring the copy to the front. Click the Make/Release Clipping Mask button in the bottom left of the Layers palette to mask the group.

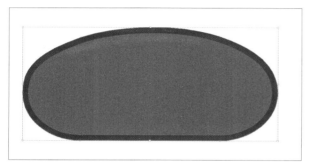

08 Now we need to add the shading around the edges of the shape. Select the background shape and **Cmd/Ctrl + C > Cmd/Ctrl + F** to copy and paste on top of itself. Knock out the fill of this new shape and change the stroke colour values to C0, M100, Y100 and K32. Thicken the stroke to 10 pixels.

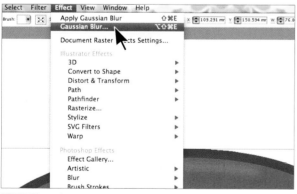

09 In the menu bar, click Effect. Don't then click Apply Gaussian Blur, as this will use the last-used settings. We want to use slightly different settings for the shading – click Gaussian Blur and set the radius to 40 pixels.

> "We need to mask the group so that any shading we apply stays within the borders of the shape"

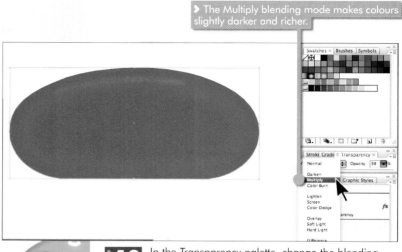

› The Multiply blending mode makes colours slightly darker and richer.

10 In the Transparency palette, change the blending mode to Multiply and reduce the opacity to 90%.

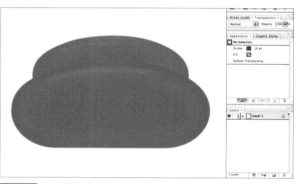

11 Double-click on an empty space to exit the group. Then, holding down **Alt/Opt + Shift**, click and drag a copy of the group directly above the original. Make it slightly smaller and place behind the original group by hitting **Cmd/Ctrl + [**.

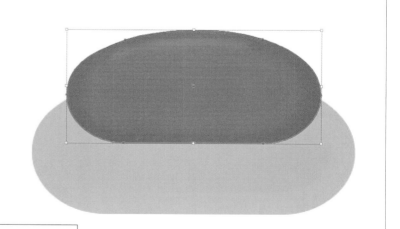

12 Double-click the new group to enter it, then select the background shape and change the fill to a deeper orange. You may find it difficult to select the background shape as the Gaussian Blur effect on the shading may overlap it: to get around this, place the shading line at the back of the group by selecting it and hitting **Cmd/Ctrl + Shift + [**, and then change the colour of the background shape, before placing it at the back again by selecting it and hitting **Cmd/Ctrl + Shift + [**.

> **LEARN** VECTOR LIQUID IMAGING

How to draw **Liquid**

Use Illustrator's Mesh and Warp tools to create a glossy water splash

Creating convincing liquid effects in vector illustration can be a tricky business. Luckily, Jing Zhang has provided us with this tutorial that shows you how to make a real splash with your art. You'll learn numerous Illustrator techniques to create vector liquid, by playing around with Illustrator's Mesh tool, Warp tool and layer blending properties.

The Mesh tool is often overlooked, but it is one of Illustrator's most powerful tools. You can use it to create realistic 3D effects and it allows you to give your work a unique finish.

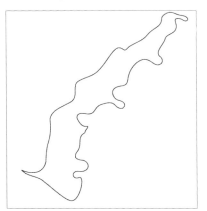

01 Fire up Illustrator and using the Pen tool (**P**), draw a basic shape of a water splash. Speed up your tracing progress by using keyboard shortcuts as you draw, such as the Selection tool (**A**), Direct Selection tool (**V**), Convert Anchor Point (**Shift + C**), Pen tool (**P**), Add Anchor Point (**+**) and Delete Anchor Point (**-**).

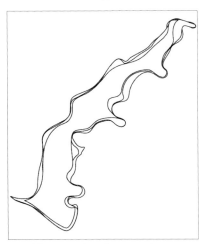

02 Copy the object you just created and use **Ctrl/Cmd + F** to paste it in the same place twice. The more layers there are, the better the effect will be. Next, click on the Warp tool (**Shift + R**) and using the default setting, warp the top and the middle layer as shown in the picture above.

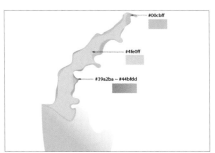

03 Colour all the objects in blue, either using the Pantone shades shown above, or by creating your own – just make sure the outer layer is in the darkest colour and the inner one the lightest.

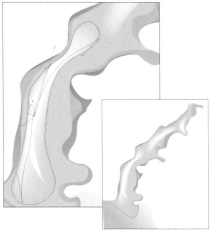

04 Next, we'll add the highlights. On the top layer, use the Pen tool (**P**) to draw up an object similar to the one shown. Try to use as few anchor points as possible to avoid complicating the mesh later. Fill the shape with the same colour as the top splash layer – the lightest blue. Using the Mesh tool (**U**), click on the centre of the highlight, and fill the anchor point with white colour. Adjust the anchor point and its arrows to make it look smooth.

Repeat this technique on the other areas of the splash, creating more highlights until your picture starts to look glossy.

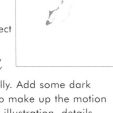

05 With the Ellipse tool (**L**), draw an ellipse object of any size. By stretching and warping the object with the Warp tool (**Shift + R**), you can 'liquefy' its shape naturally. Add some dark twisted strokes to make up the motion of the splash. In illustration, details define the quality, so it's definitely worth taking more time over this step.

06 Still with the Ellipse tool (**L**) selected, create a few water drops of various transparencies. As real water drops are rarely uniform in shape use the Warp tool (**Shift + R**) again to make them look more realistic. ❯

STEP 07 Select a few of the main water drops and make them more solid with the Mesh Tool (**U**), using the method described in Step 4. You can even change the colour some of the anchor points to a darker shadow colour.

STEP 08 Composition is crucial, particularly in a piece with lots of natural elements, so be careful not to overdo any particular sections. Here, I've given prominence to the right-hand side of the splash, where the water pours.

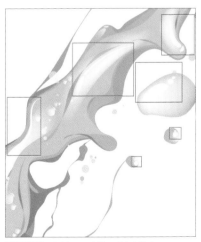

STEP 09 Add sparkling highlights to your splash as shown here. Vary the opacity of each highlight shape from 50% to 95%. This subtle detail will dramatically improve the texture's appearance.

STEP 10 To create the Koi, I used the help of a plug-in called SymmetryWorks to make the fish scales. You don't need the plug-in to make them, but it saves a lot of time! You can either download it from *artlandia.com/products/SymmetryWorks* and follow my settings as shown above, or you can create your own. Then, with your pattern selected, go to **Object > Expand**.

STEP 11 Draw a Koi and duplicate the body shape, using one as a mask for the fish scale (**Ctrl/Cmd + 7**). Colour the other parts with gradient colour. With luck, your Koi carp should look similar to the one here on the right.

STEP 12 To make the fish look solid, duplicate its body and fill it with darker blue colour. Next, apply the Mesh tool (**U**) and, using the same method as described in Steps 4 and 7, add an anchor point in the middle, and fill it with white. Click on Opacity in the menu bar and set the blending mode to Multiply in the drop-down menu.

STEP 13 To add extra highlights to the fish, use the Pen tool (**P**) to draw a blue shape, repeat the Mesh tool method and fill the middle anchor point with white colour. Finally, change the blending mode to Lighten.

Copy and paste the Koi carp to different areas and vary their size and rotation. Use the layer stack to place them in front and behind the water.

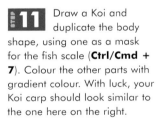

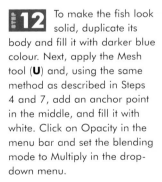

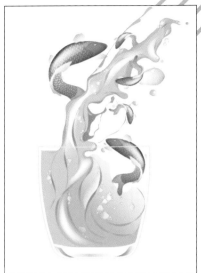

STEP 14 We're almost there, so lets add in the glass now. Use the Pen tool (**P**) to draw the outline of a glass with a stroke weight of about 3pt.

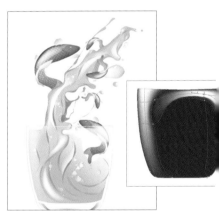

STEP 15 Finally, duplicate the glass object but close the path, and fill it with dark grey. Use the Mesh tool (**U**) to add a few anchor points. Change the colour of some of the anchor points to white.

Next, change the blending mode to Screen and set the opacity to 69%. Save this as a new layer at the top of the stack. I've included some additional elements in my finished design – fruit slices and ice – so why not add your own touches? ∎

PROFILE JING ZHANG

> Originally from China, London-based creative designer and illustrator Jing makes her living by doing things she loves. She works for clients including *Lonely Planet*, Ford, Osiris, and more.

CONTACT
• *mazakii.com*

STEP 12 Now we're really getting there. To finish off I'm adding a few wavy lines over the edges of the tile to help the pattern flow a little better, using the same technique that we used on the river. Select the area that falls outside the tile with the Direct Selection tool (**A**) then Cut (**Cmd/Ctrl + X**) and paste (**Cmd/Ctrl + V**) this on the opposite side of the tile, using the smart guides to line it up. Now when you place two tiles they will align.

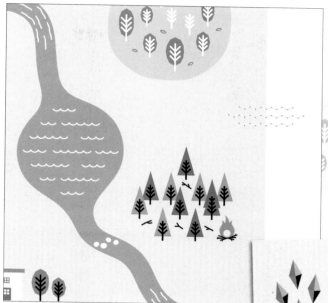

> Add to the fantastical appeal of your map – and have a bit of fun – by adding in a few quirky creatures here and there.

STEP 13 To make the artwork really sing, it requires a bit more personality – literally. I've added some of my signature characters to add charm to the piece. Add creatures of your own here.

STEP 14 Now you have your finished tile, copy and paste the original and line up the corners to match. You now have a pattern that tiles indefinitely and can be made as big as you like, ready for use as a poster, fabric print or anything you fancy. ∎

INFO ANDREW GROVES

Above "This is a repeat pattern that I had printed onto fabric. I used many of the techniques in my tutorial to create this pattern."

Left "This is a personal illustration called The Lake Keeper. It was created to be sold as a gallery print through Society6.com."

> Working under the name Imakethings, Andrew Groves is a freelance illustrator. He says: "I have a particular interest in the natural world, and aim to invent characters that explore the grotesque beauty of its many beasts and creatures, and the folklore that surrounds them."

Andrew is currently based in the UK creating work for clients such as Foundation Skateboards, *Snowboarder Magazine*, Orange and Panasonic to name but a few. He is also constantly involved in self-initiated projects and schemes as well as creating work for exhibitions and shows worldwide.

CONTACT
• *imakethings.co.uk*

TIME TO COMPLETE
• 2 hours

SOFTWARE
• Adobe Illustrator

PROJECT FILES
• Files for this tutorial are downloadable from *theartistsguide.co.uk/ downloads*

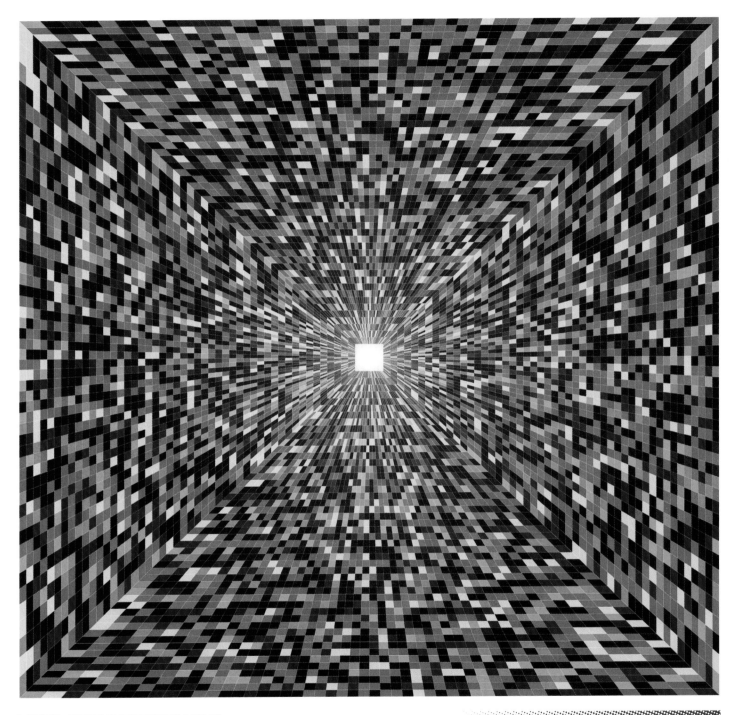

> **LEARN** REPEATING PATTERN TECHNIQUES

Design a geometric retro poster

Create a complex op-art design with ease using scripts and InDesign CS5's new layout tools

his tutorial explains how to create one of Simon C Page's seemingly complicated posters via some nifty tricks in Illustrator and InDesign CS5. Like most of his more intricate designs, he created this using Flash Professional CS5's

ActionScript language – but here he shows you how to do it in Illustrator, using that application's ExtendScript toolkit.

This part of the tutorial should give you enough to get you up and running with some basic scripting and an appetite to see the host

of styles you can create with scripts – styles that would take you countless hours to replicate by hand.

You'll then learn how to take this artwork and turn it into a poster, drawing on the styles of classic 1950s book covers.

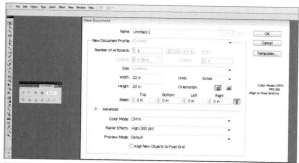

01 The first step is to create the main framework for this artwork, which is created out of a very large number of concentric squares and lines rotated round into a circle. This design is going to be square, but there is no reason you couldn't replicate it with a circle or rectangle, for example.

The artwork needs to be 22 x 22 inches square, and so the first square to draw should be around 21 x 21 inches, giving you a nice one-inch border. Make sure you leave the black 1pt border on, this will also be useful later on.

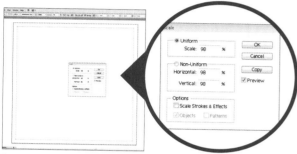

02 Centre this square on the document and, while selecting it, bring up the Scale dialog box (**Object > Transform > Scale**). From this enter 98% and then select Copy. This will then create a centred copy of the square at 98% of its size. Select the Transform Again function for this second square (**Cmd/Ctrl + D**) to duplicate this. Hold the keys down to repeat this until the square look very dark in the centre. Zoom in and remove any squares that have overlapping borders.

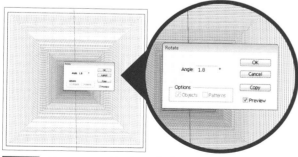

03 Now we need to do a similar technique but with a line. Create a new layer and add a 1pt black line down the middle of the page. Now bring up the Rotate dialog (**Object > Transform > Rotate**). We want 200 lines, which equates to a 1.8° rotation on each to make a circle.

> INFO

TIME TO COMPLETE
• 45 minutes

SOFTWARE
• Adobe Illustrator CS5, InDesign CS5

PROJECT FILES
• Files for this tutorial are downloadable from *theartistsguide.co.uk/downloads*

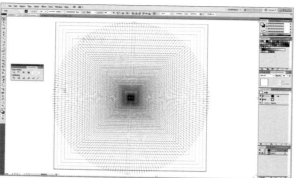

04 Enter 1.8° in the dialog box and again select the Copy button, which will leave the original line but also creates a copy that has been transformed with a 1.8° rotation. Select this new line and hit (**Cmd/Ctrl + D**) repeatedly to run the 'Transform Again' function until you have made a complete circle.

SCALE IT UP

> If you don't want a white block in the middle section, experiment with increasing the 98% scale amount to one that fits the centre of the design better.

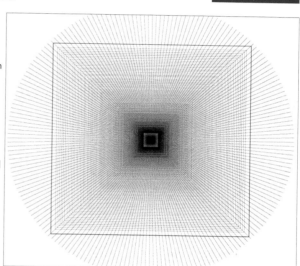

05 Ensure that all the contents of both layers are centred on the document, and that the lines from the second layer all overlap outside of the document edge. Hit Select All (**Cmd/Ctrl + A**) and make sure the Line and Fill properties of all objects are transparent.

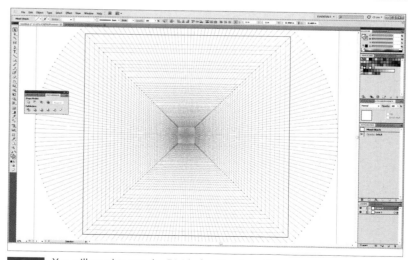

06 You will need to use the Divide function from the Pathfinder tool (**Cmd/Ctrl + Shift + F9**) to divide up where these objects cross over. When you are doing more complicated dividing, it's worth noting that the Pathfinder window has a dialog that allows you to change the level of precision and removal of redundant points. **>**

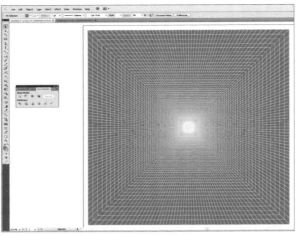

07 The next step is to fill all of these objects with a seemingly random pattern of colours. Doing this with the current framework will end up with a bunch of irregular shapes in centre of the design that don't match. For the cleanest look, remove these by selecting them from the centre and deleting.

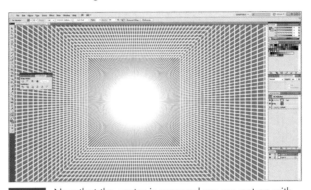

08 Now that the centre is removed we can get on with painting all the thousands of elements randomly, with a set of colours based on a swatch. Here I am using a palette of purple, pink, red, orange and yellow.

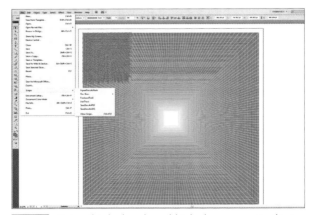

09 Doing this by hand would take hours or even days, but using Illustrator's scripting capabilities we can reduce this to mere minutes. Select all the objects and then select **File > Scripting > Other Script** and load *Random_ Fill_With_Swatch_Time_Curve.jsx*. If you have a high-end desktop this will take a few minutes to execute. However, if you are running this on a laptop, simply select just a few objects at a time and run the script on each in turn to complete the entire set of objects. To learn how this script works, see **Follow the script** (left). To finish off the design, select all and give it a 0.5pt white border line – and there you have it.

10 We now want to turn this piece of art into an A2 poster print. Open InDesign CS5 and create a new document with the dimensions of our output size – in our case 360 (width) x 554 (depth), ready to be produced in sheets and cut to size at our print house. Leave the other settings as they are.

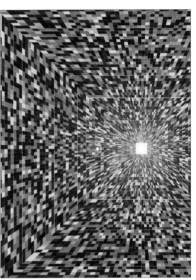

11 Draw out a frame from the top left margin corner across and down towards the bottom of the right margin, leaving space between the bottom of the frame and the bottom margin for our text. Ours is 334.427 x 495.017mm.

Select **File > Place** (or **Cmd/Ctrl + D**) and select your artwork. As the artwork is square and this is a portrait poster, we'll need to crop some off while still maintaining its symmetrical structure. First, right-click on the image and select **Fitting > Fill Frame Proportionally**.

Move your mouse over the image, and a semi-transparent doughnut will appear. This is the new Content Grabber, which allows you to do many of the functions of the Direct Selection Tool using the standard Selection Tool. Hold **Shift** to allow movement in only one direction, grab the doughnut and drag to the left so the images moves within the frame. Move it until the pink vertical line tells you it's in the centre.

STEP 12 The artwork would look better against black, so draw out a text frame that extends beyond the document frame (to allow for bleed) and fill it with a rich black (C40, M40, Y40 and K100). We could put this in the back using **Cmd/Ctrl + Shift + [**, but it's time to check out InDesign CS5's new Photoshop-style Layers palette. Each object becomes a sub-layer, so it's best to learn how to use this with only a few layers.

Select the Layers panel (**F7**) and open Layer 1. Click on the <text frame> layer, click again and change its name to *Black Background*. Drag this layer below the main artwork.

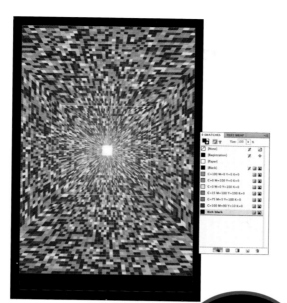

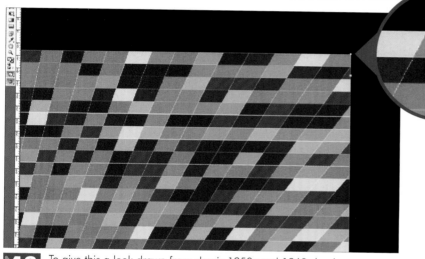

STEP 13 To give this a look drawn from classic 1950s and 1960s book covers, we're breaking out the rounded corners. Zoom so you can see the top right corner close up. Select the main artwork and click on the yellow box on the right of the frame. This opens up the corners for editing. Grab the yellow triangle that's appeared on the top of the frame and drag it to the left to curve the corner. Pull it out to 4.233mm. This affects all corners – if you want to affect just one, hold down **Shift** when dragging.

TIME CURVE #3
an exploration of creativity

CREATED USING ADOBE ILLUSTRATOR CS5
FLASH PROFESSIONAL CS5 & INDESIGN CS5

DigitalArts

STEP 14 To add more of book-cover influence, add some measured typography in the space at the bottom to complete its stylish appearance. ■

PROFILE SIMON C PAGE

> Simon C Page is a self-taught graphic designer from the UK. He loves many aspects of design but his main passions are typography art, illustration and geometric design.

"I would find it hard to choose a favourite," he says "and often I will try and combine these creative fields in to my design work."

Simon likes his work to evolve naturally and not stay too static. He often challenges myself with new self-initiated works for his website, regularly showing variations in his creative process.

CONTACT
• *simoncpage.co.uk*

Two posters created for last year's International Year of Astronomy.

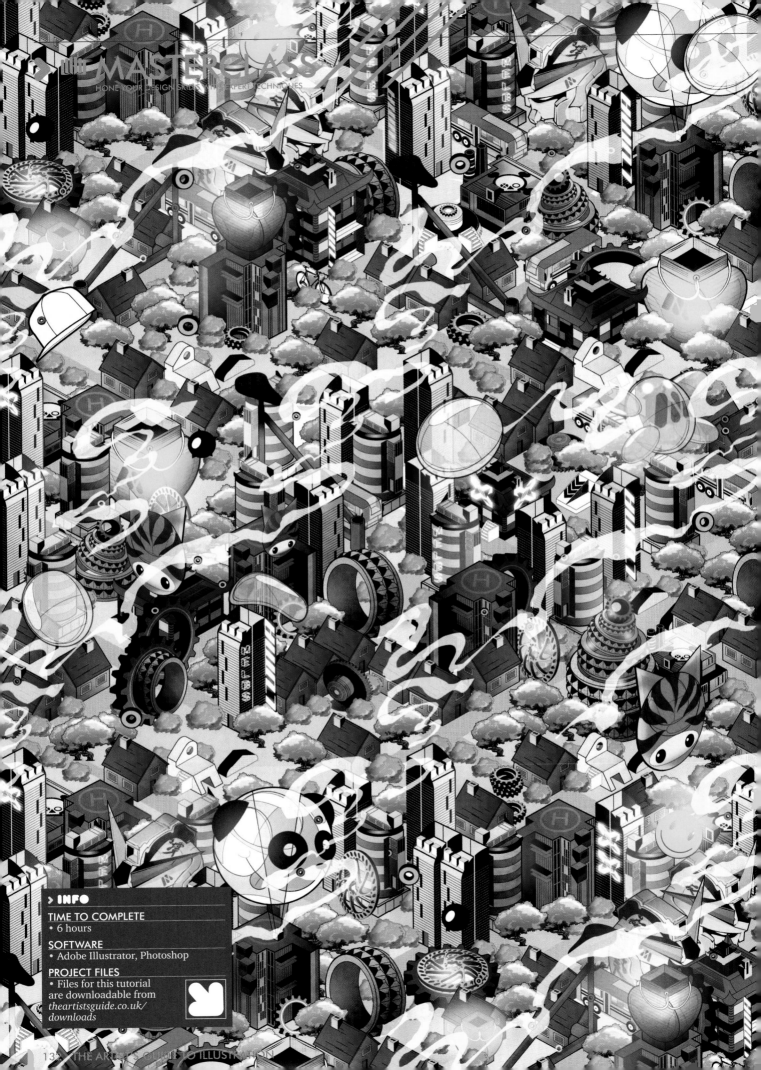

> **INFO**

TIME TO COMPLETE
• 6 hours

SOFTWARE
• Adobe Illustrator, Photoshop

PROJECT FILES
• Files for this tutorial
are downloadable from
*theartistsguide.co.uk/
downloads*

Build an entire city out of tiled elements

You can easily combine isometrically drawn objects with repeat tiling to create a complex cityscape, as **2xanadu** demonstrates

It was two years ago that the design agency 2xanadu used an isometric grid to create a repeat pattern for a bike frame made by Hong Kong company Luma. Now they've repeated the trick to create the city on the left, which will appear on Luma cycling apparel and gear.

Isometric grids are a great way to achieve a 3D/2D look. Couple them with a repeat pattern and you can achieve some striking effects.

01 The isometric grid is a useful tool for drawing objects in perspective. It's formed of vertical lines plus lines at 60° to either side, all meeting at common points to form a web of equilateral triangles (*right*). We've provided one in the project files – an Illustrator document named *Grid.ai*.

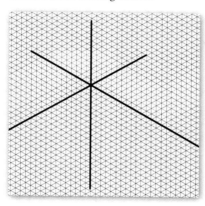

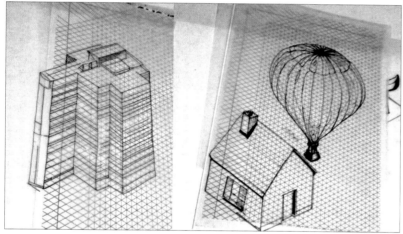

02 Like every great idea, our city begins in the sketchbook or layout pad, with a printout of the grid under the top sheet. Sketch some elements and scan them in.

03 Import the grid into a new Illustrator document and lock the layer. Now place one of your scans over it in a separate layer and set the opacity to 70%, so that the grid can be seen underneath.

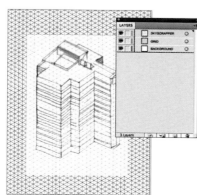

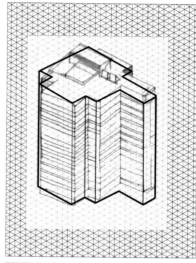

04 Start drawing with the Pen tool (**P**). Join all paths up – there should be no overhanging bits. Keep it clean and use the grid to achieve straight lines at 30° to the horizontal.

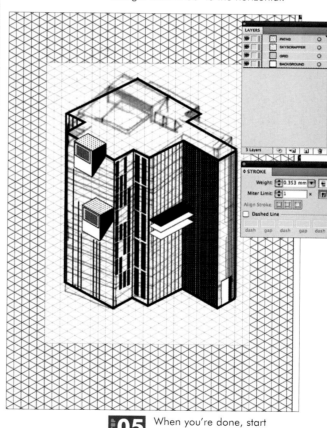

05 When you're done, start adding some fine details. Remember that this will be a repeat pattern and that it will be a small part of a much bigger canvas, so you don't need to go mad. Just use different weights of stroke and simple shapes to create depth and detail. ➤

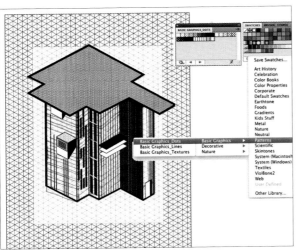

INTRIGUINGLY RANDOM

> When you've practically finished building your cityscape, try scattering a few extra objects about the pattern to create a more intricate and intriguing look.

06 We want the overall look to be sharp and very graphic, so use the built-in halftone black-and-white swatches (accessed from the Swatch panel or using **Window > Swatch Libraries > Patterns > Basic Graphics**).

07 Once you're happy with all your elements, make sure they're grouped individually, then copy each one and paste it into Photoshop.

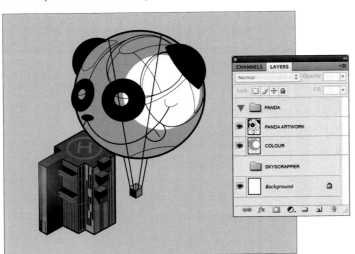

08 In Photoshop, put each element in its own layer group. Within each group, create a new layer beneath the element and call it 'Colour'. Set the element layer's blending mode to Multiply, then go to the Colour layer and start colouring it in.

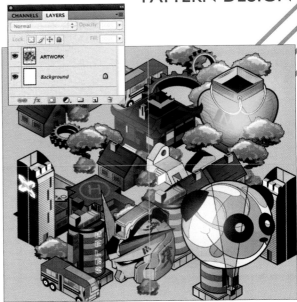

09 Once all your elements are finished, start composing the central part of your cityscape. When you're happy with your work, go to **Layer > Flatten image**.

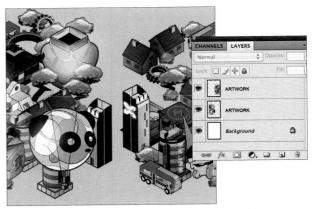

10 Now slice the image into two from top to bottom. Move the left half to the far right of the document, and the right half to the far left.

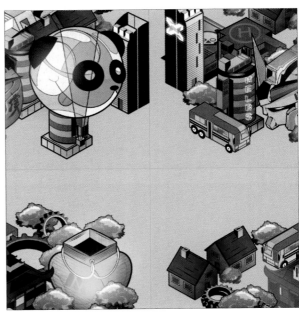

11 Slice the image into two from left to right this time. Put the bottom half up against the top of the document, and move the top half down to the bottom.

12 You will be left with a space in the centre. Fill it in with the rest of your elements, but don't go over the edges of the empty space, or you'll compromise the repeat pattern which you'll create in Step 14.

13 Flatten the image again and tweak the overall look using **Image > Adjustments > Levels**. Now paint a neon-glow look over certain areas with a soft brush at 70% opacity and the mode set to Screen.

14 Flatten the image again. Now select all and copy and paste, and start creating your tiling.

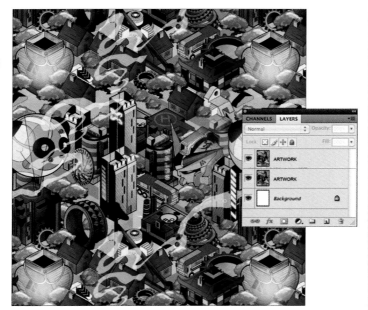

15 To give the pattern a more random feel, we've actually used four tiles with some small variations – we've moved buildings around, added stuff and taken stuff away. This yields a more diverse and arresting look than a strict repetition of the pattern. Finally, we boosted the brightness to improve its impact. ■

Above top Peter Lin of 2xanadu blended Eastern and Western influences to design the graphics on this bike frame.

Above Focus Bikes commissioned this design, in the colours of German professional cycling team Milram, for their Hong Kong showroom.

CHAPTER 7

TYPE ART

TURN LETTERFORMS INTO STUNNING ILLUSTRATIONS

WORDS GRAEME AYMER

Type
art
now

Creatives are putting elaborate lettering at the heart of illustrations. Welcome to the new wave of type-based art

It's hard to miss the current vogue for illustration-based ads and other projects – but even more noticeable at the moment is a trend for putting text front and centre, integrating it into the very fabric of the image in detailed, elaborate artworks.

Advertisers have largely led the trend, first by embracing illustration as a handy way of helping a sceptical public rekindle its love affairs with their products when photos just make the public even more dubious.

Illustration helps some advertisers dodge regulators and ease the responses of a critical public. For instance, in 2005, guidelines for advertising alcohol in the UK changed, and it became impossible to show sexy people having a good time while drinking alcohol. How do you make your brand fun without showing people having fun while using it? Stella Artois went with a well-received illustration-based campaign for its beers.

Mid-decade, faced with a public that was increasingly anti-junk food and anti-corporate, Coca-Cola turned to illustration for its 'The Coke Side of Life' campaign. And of course, where the big junk food and alcohol brands lead, the rest follow.

Once advertisers had embraced illustration as a mainstream strategy, it was a relatively short leap to illustration-based type. Look at AMV BBDO's bold ads for *The Economist*, or Alex Trochut's recent work for beer brand Estrella Damm. In these campaigns, the words aren't separate from the image. They are the image, or at least an essential element of it.

Why words?

The shift to type-based art is partly a way of keeping illustration-led ads fresh. Technology has a part to play, too: try using your old G4 PowerBook to do some of the serious heavy lifting you now do on your MacBook Pro.

Most obviously, though, it offers a way for advertisers to marry a clear verbal message and an illustration, presenting a slogan or message in a more intriguing and engaging manner than straight-up text.

Letters are often mashed up and mixed up, glooped up and obscured. Rendered large, for example on a large-scale poster at a train platform, they invite the viewer to engage with the illustration – and its message. On a magazine cover or CD poster, the effect is the same.

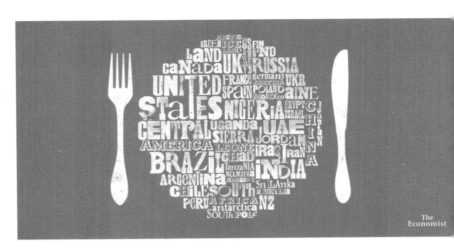

"Type-based art presents a slogan or message in a more engaging way than straight-up text"

Type-based art is also a fantastic way to make a message unique. You can use customised or one-off fonts – this is a particularly handy connotation for brands whose message rests on customisation and tailored solutions for clients, such as mobile phone service providers.

Typographic illustration is full of potential for graphic designers, then – but it's a "double-edged sword", according to designer Craig Ward. "For one, you're restricted by the fact you have to use type – but then, conversely, that's ❯

Top and **right** AMV/BBDO's ads for *The Economist* by Craig Ward (top) and Non Format (right) integrate the message into images with trademark wit.

Far right *Diagonal*, by Alex Trochut.

no more restricting than a brief coming in saying 'we need a picture of a guy sat at a desk'," Ward explains. "It's just something else as a subject matter and it can be embellished in any way you like. That for me is the most appealing thing: that [with typographic illustration] I'm not tied to any one particular style."

In fact, that restriction is its charm. Illustrating with type enables you to push the envelope, to distort and twist letterforms beyond what you can do in terms of traditional typography. Yet an A still has to look like an A, and a B, a B. That's a fascinating conundrum for many creatives.

"The vast majority of clients are too interested in legibility. People find it interesting to figure it out"

Marian Bantjes

Below Seb Lester has moved from lettering design into type-based art, creating pieces including this editorial design for *Wired* (**left**) and a series of limited-edition prints (**right**).

But just how much like an A does an A have to look? "The vast majority of clients are far too interested in exact legibility," says Canadian designer Marian Bantjes (*bantjes.com*). "I think people find it interesting to see something that's intriguing. It's debatable whether there's an advantage to being able to read, 'Sale On Washing Machines $999!' in Helvetica or having to figure that out."

"I'm a commercial artist," counters London-based Radim Malinic, who designs as Brand Nu (*brandnu.co.uk*). "Legibility in a commercial project is the main point. If the client doesn't read it, the customer doesn't read it and there's no point in doing it."

"I think it depends on the application," argues Barcelona-based designer Alex Trochut, currently the poster boy for lettering-based illustration. "If you're designing a billboard, people will only have a second to read it. If you have a record cover that people could spend time with, you can be less readable."

Your clients will probably influence where you stand on the debate. But be clear on one thing: without a clear voice, a creative vision, and something interesting to say

Above London designer Radim Malinic of Brand Nu created the branding for the Creativity in Conflict student competition.

creatively, you'll be little more than an also-ran. Beware of what Marian Bantjes calls "ornament barf".

"I'm less concerned with some shaky kerning than I am with the fact that there's a hundred or more designers out there just trying to out-Trochut Alex Trochut," says Craig Ward, when asked about the style's danger zones. "Even he would concede that his work doesn't apply to everything and – more – that's just one small facet of his style."

Getting started

Do you need to master font-design to dabble in type-based art? Not necessarily. Alex Trochut readily admits his own font, Neo Deco, features little in the way of kerning. Similarly, Radim Malinic is not a typeface designer. Others, such as London's Seb Lester or Brooklyn's Jessica Hische, almost always create their own lettering – but then, they're both experienced typographers.

It's more important to take the time to understand how type works, both in terms of white space and letter proportion. Check out a few books, such as Wilson Harvey's *1000 Type Treatments*, or *Type: v. 2: A Visual History of Typefaces and Graphic Styles* by Alston Purvis and Cees de Jong.

Popular tastes change over time: flares get replaced by skinny jeans, which get replaced by flares again. Clients may decide that typographic illustration is no longer 'in' over the next few years. However, working with letters will always remain creatively satisfying and interesting.

As Seb Lester remarks: "There's a whole wealth of untapped typographic styles that you can draw from – and a rich legacy of over 2,000 years of Latin lettering styles for inspiration." ∎

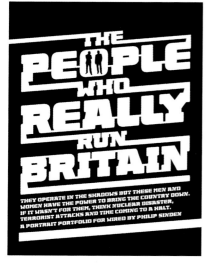

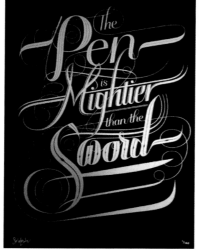

the one that got away

> Craig Ward's ambitious typography project for the New York Art Directors Club took some unexpected directions.

"The typeface was created specifically for the ADC piece"

Craig Ward

Former Londoner Craig Ward has amassed an eye-grabbing portfolio of type-based illustration for the likes of BMW, the *Economist* and Nike. Online, he's better known as Words Are Pictures, but in the real world, he's a senior designer and typographer at New York studio Grey.

One of his most ambitious projects was for the Art Directors Club of New York, for whom he designed its Young Guns 7 logo for 2009's recipients of the prestigious award. "Of course they had no money, but the scale of the project really appealed to me so I took it on," he explains. "Basically they wanted a logo that incorporated the letters A, D and C, Young Guns, the number 7 and a cube – a reference to the award you get."

Ward and the Art Directors Club agreed on the idea of Chinese tangrams – ancient geometric puzzles – that could be reordered into the required figures, with Craig even designing a typeface around the idea. With a view to animating the figures in 3D, Craig went as far as learning Cinema 4D, and even an iPhone app was mooted.

However, things didn't quite pan out that way. The scope of the ideas far exceeded the budget, so the idea ended up as one element of the overall publicity campaign. Despite this, the project shows that typographic illustration can be ambitious, moving far beyond the idea of just ornamenting letterforms.

"I was definitely trying to do something different for this project, so they really got the works," he says. "I did a custom font, used colours that were nothing like anything else I've done. The typeface was created specifically for the piece and drawn around the grid I created for the tangram itself."

wordsarepictures.co.uk

Top The Hirsutura typeface was created for a personal project.

Above right and far right Letterforms and artworks created for the Art Directors Club of New York.

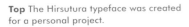

Left Trochut's Barcelona-inspired Estrella Dam poster.

Above A piece for If You Could exhibition, answering the question, "if you could do anything in 2008, what would it be?"

Right Front and back (inset) covers for *Varoom*.

Letters that sink in

> **Alex Trochut's liquid type added va-va-voom to London art journal *Varoom*.**

For a long time Alex Trochut's designs for Barcelona beer brand Estrella Damm were regular sights on billboards in British cities, and for many creatives, particularly type-based artists, he is quite simply 'the man'.

He describes his Estrella posters, the illustrated shapes and their featured letter forms as being influenced by Barcelona – its atmosphere, its fantastical architecture and a vibrant artistic legacy left by Gaudí, Miró and Dalí, among others.

Trochut's work for London art title *Varoom* caught our eye. The magazine commissioned him to create an illustration-based cover for its November 2009 issue. Art-directed by Non Format, the idea was to create a two-part illustration (for both front and back covers) in which the line 'This Is Illustration' would be written in liquid and gradually sink into another liquid.

"We wanted to make the liquid look as fluid as possible so it would look like a splash that was natural," Trochut explains.

"If you push to express yourself, you're forgetting how you communicate"

Alex Trochut

This gave him a lot of leeway for the letter design. The idea was to create something more illustration-based than typographical. Legibility wasn't a key concern. However, it was important that letters were in proportion, that they didn't look 'wrong'. Therefore he looked at flowing type, such as the font Candy, as well as lettering from the 1970s for an understanding of the necessary strokes necessary for the right look.

For Trochut, this proportionality is vital. "It's like a hydraulic system: if you push a lot to express yourself, then you're forgetting the way you communicate," he says. "Everybody will see how beautiful the shapes can be, but maybe just a few people will be able to read it. It's important to find that middle point, where you can be as expressive as you want and most people can read it, too." ***alextrochut.com***

Experiment with typography effects

Create a trendy logo using traditional and digital media

There's no doubt about it, London is hip. In this tutorial Holland-based designer Bram Vanhaeren shows his admiration by creating a new piece that draws on all that's great about the city – taking inspiration from the Olympics, underground club scenes, and the vista from up high.

This masterclass is about giving your typography illustration a fresh touch and experimenting with traditional and digital media, mixing patterns and textures to give your work an extra personal spark. For this tutorial you will need basic Illustrator and Photoshop skills, as well as some watercolour paint.

Afterwards, you should have acquired hands-on techniques you can use on work ranging from typography and editorial to photo manipulation.

MAKING YOUR OWN BRUSHES

> When creating brushes in Photoshop, make sure that your background is white and check the levels to make sure there's enough contrast without losing quality. Find the right balance before turning them into Photoshop brushes.

01 Open a new document in Illustrator. Type your text with any font you like – I chose Avant Garde Bold. Select your text and go to **Type > Create Outlines**. Now you can adjust each letter separately.

02 Move your text around until it's sitting in the position you want. I placed some red squares, which helped me to line the text up, and removed them once I found the right composition.

03 To complete the typography, connect the letters using the Pen tool (**P**) to draw the connection you desire. In this case we just need a couple of oblique rectangles. You can use Pathfinder to merge them all together. Now we have our finished typography to work with.

04 In this Step we're going to add a fade effect on some of our letters. First, create two white triangles. Take the Pen tool (**P**), and create a triangle with flat side on top, and sharp side downwards. Duplicate this shape and place the triangles straddling one side of the letter.

> The Blend effect, combined with triangular shapes, forms this repeated pattern.

05 Go to **Object > Blend > Blend Options > Specified Steps > 20**. Press **W** to use the Blend tool and click on both triangles. It should render the result immediately.

06 Experiment with this technique, using different kinds of shapes to create unique shading in your vector-based illustrations. This is my result.

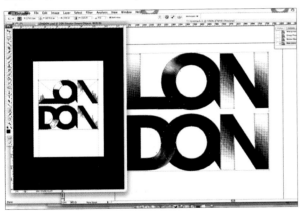

07 Open a new document in Photoshop by hitting **Cmd/Ctrl + N** – if you plan to get this printed later, try an A3 or A2 file at 300dpi. If you just want to experiment, keep it at 800 x 600 pixels and 72dpi resolution. I always start with a dirty paper texture background, to give it an extra touch. Drag your work from Illustrator to your Photoshop document and Rasterize your vector layer (in the Layer menu).

08 Select your text by holding **Cmd/Ctrl** and clicking on the layer in the Layers palette. Copy this selection and paste it to the background texture layer to get rid of the white background. Your typography should now be part of the texture. Change the Blend Mode to Multiply, so the white parts disappear in the background. This must be done in Photoshop because the blending mode we've chosen means we can't remove the triangles from the text with the Pathfinder.

A SECOND GLANCE

> After spending more than two to three hours on a piece, take a break and return to your work later, so you can have a fresh new look at it. You might be surprised with what crazy ideas you come up with. Enjoy and have fun.

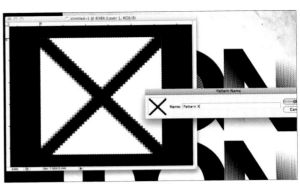

09 For the next Step we're going to make a new pattern. In Photoshop, open a new document at 50 x 50 pixels with a transparent or white background. Make a cross with the Line tool (**U**). Next, hit **Cmd/Ctrl + A** to select all and **Edit > Define Pattern**. I have a lot of patterns to play with: big crosses, small crosses, dots, lines, squares and so on – they're all very useful. Also try more lines and other shapes to create patterns.

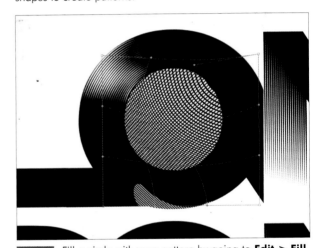

10 Fill a circle with your pattern by going to **Edit > Fill** and selecting your pattern. Go to **Edit > Transform > Warp** and pull on a corner to add depth. Place this behind some of your letters. Play with your options to come up with a good solution.

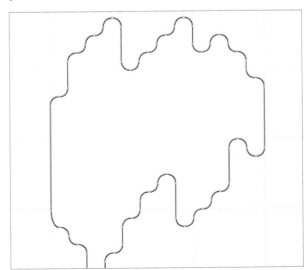

11 At the moment we don't have much colour. To fix this, I made a shape in Illustrator with the Pen tool (**P**), which I will use as a base to create some extra colour by adding gradients and textures.

> For a more washed-out feel, create a merged version of all layers, apply a Gaussian blur to it and duplicate the result

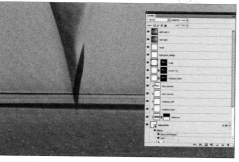

14 Adding a twist to the bottom of the 'v' reflects the twist at the tops of the 'd' and 'i' nicely. To do this, copy the tip from the 'd' and 'i', flip it vertically and paste it behind the tip of the 'v'. Change the colour of the tip to brown to match it with the image.

PROFILE CHARLES WILLIAMS
> Charles Williams is an award-winning illustrator. He produces type and illustration for clients such as Volkswagen, the BBC, Nike and Adobe. He also spends as much time as possible on experimental work. Charles has exhibited recently in London and elsewhere in Europe, and has been featured in several type and illustration books, magazines and type/illustration/design blogs. Resident in London, he works under the moniker Made Up.

CONTACT
• madeup.org

12 Select all of your layers, copy a merged version (**Cmd/Ctrl + Shift + C**) and paste it at the top of the layer stack. Apply a Gaussian Blur at 60% and set the layer's blending mode to Soft Light at 60% opacity. If you want a more washed-out, retro feel, duplicate this layer.

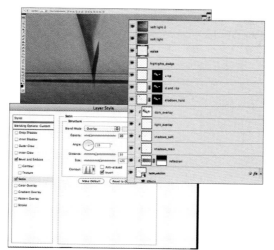

15 Create a layer and drag it above all other layers. Fill it with white and set its blending mode to multiply. Add Noise at 20% and desaturate the layer (**Cmd/Ctrl + Shift + U**). Add some soft Satin to the 'type_vector' layer by selecting **Layer > Layer Style > Satin**, using the values in the screenshot.

13 One very important element that will help integrate the type into the scenes is to add a shadow to the ground. Select the type, then create a layer above the 'desert' layer set to Multiply and 60% opacity.

Fill in the selection with black, and flip the shape vertically. Now Free Transform it so it is long and thin. Add a Gaussian Blur of 30%. Apply a mask and use a black brush to fade the shadow out on the right.

16 To complete the work, add some colour adjustment layers to bring out the yellows and the reds. ■

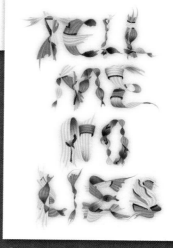

Above top Nike Ribbons.
Above centre Just Say No.
Above Tell Me No Lies.

01 The simplest way to create great typography is to modify and embellish lettering created with an existing font. Here we'll take advantage of a typeface called CAC Pinafore, available for free at *bit.ly/gF4xBt*. In a new A4 portrait Illustrator document, type the text 'You Are Sweet as Sugar' in this font at 150pt. Centre-align the text, then convert it into outlines (**Cmd/Ctrl + Shift + O**).

02 Perhaps surprisingly for a free font, CAC Pinafore does have a very appealing flow to it — but nevertheless we're about to alter some of the letters to give them a more hand-drawn look. Using the Brush tool (**B**), redo the letters highlighted in red, then replace the original letters with the ones you've made, making sure to cover any joins.

> **LEARN** FLUID TYPE EFFECTS

Type that's fit to eat

Radim Malinic creates a message to tempt any chocoholic

Exercising creative freedom can be a difficult balancing act. Occasionally you'll have all the time you need to finish a project, but at other times the speediest turnaround will be of the essence.

Regardless of the time available, your work always has to hit the mark, bettering whatever you did previously. So it's imperative to know when you can take a prudent shortcut and when only the utmost care will make your illustration look perfect.

This tutorial reflects some of that dilemma. Here Radim Malinic shows you how to create the semblance of words spelt out in melted chocolate. You'll be encouraged to speed up at times, while at other times you'll need to linger over tiny details to create that ultra-realistic look, fit for any advertising campaign or logo.

The results should look better than Heston Blumenthal could achieve. And you won't need an ounce of chocolate.

> **INFO**

TIME TO COMPLETE
• 5 hours

SOFTWARE
• Illustrator & Photoshop CS5

PROJECT FILES
• Files for this tutorial are downloadable from *theartistsguide.co.uk/downloads*

03 Apply a 4pt stroke around the text to make it look bolder. The type also needs to look more fluid, so let's join up some of the parts and add a few embellishments, including extended terminals on the two capital S's, swooping ligatures to tie the letters together better and looping tails at the end of each word.

Create a few quick swirly strokes with the Brush tool to see how they fit together. Select each of these, open the Brushes panel (**F5**) and click on the Remove Brush Stroke button so we can adjust the paths as if we'd created them with the Pen or Pencil tool.

04 When you're happy with the positioning of each stroke, go to the Stroke panel (**F10**), change the stroke width to 11pt and also hit the Round Cap button. This will make all the new elements appear similar to the original typeface.

That done, use the Width tool (**Shift + W**) to enlarge or shrink the tips of some lines to give these curly strokes a slightly more varied look. Repeat the process for all joins to emulate a hand-drawn look once again.

05 Copy and paste some of the looping tails you've just created and place them around the type. Adjust their shape to fit with the type by using the Direct Selection Tool (**A**) and moving curves as desired.

Next, we'll turn everything into one element so it's easier to work with when we add colour and shading. First, select all and hit **Object > Path > Outline Stroke** to turn all elements into filled shapes. Select all again, go to the Pathfinder panel (**Cmd/Ctrl + Shift + F9**) and select Unite. Clean up any imperfections by deleting anchor points.

06 To create the area that we'll add inner-glow-style highlights to, go to **Object > Path > Offset Path** and use -0.85mm as the Offset. Cut this offset path out and paste it next to the main type. The result should look like what's in the project file *Type.ai*.

07 Invert the fill and stroke colours (**Shift + X**) and add a 4pt stroke to the shape. Next, we'll create the flowing elements that will be composited onto the main text to make it look like viscous chocolate, so we need to think about how this will work.

The approach we'll use is to cut out lines from the outline to give a sense of motion to the type. Use the Direct Selection tool (**A**) and delete parts of the lines and the tails – basically, those areas that would be touched lightly by a brush if you really were painting with melted chocolate. You can achieve this by going to the Stroke panel and selecting Width Profile 1 in the Profile drop-down menu. This will give you lines that are thin at the ends and heavy in the middle.

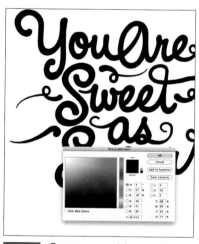

08 Create a new A4 portrait CMYK document in Photoshop. Copy and paste in your original, filled text, selecting Shape Layer in the Paste dialog box. This keeps it as a vector element, making any subsequent scaling much quicker and easier to do.

Double-click on the Shape Layer's layer thumbnail in the Layers panel and change the colour to C56, M89, Y83 and K74 for that genuine chocolatey look. Name this layer 'Type'.

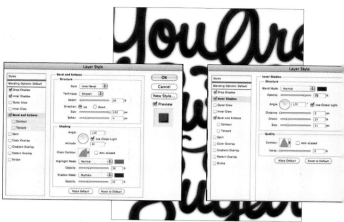

09 To give our main shape a three-dimensional look, we will use blending modes to emboss the type, along with inner shadows. Double-click on the 'Type' layer's name to bring up the Layer Style panel and set up the Bevel and Emboss and Inner Shadows effects as shown above.

10 Now we will bring in the flowing elements part of our Illustrator document. Paste it on the top of the main object and set the opacity to 30%. Change this element's colour to a dark brown to match the colour of the type behind it. Call this layer 'Flow'.

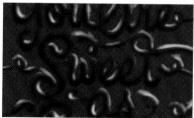

11 We'll now apply highlights to make it look as if the lighting is coming from one source in the top right. Select the Brush tool, go to the Brush Presets panel and select a Soft Round brush with opacity and flow both set to 10%, and with Shape Dynamics and Airbrush turned on. Make a selection from the 'Type' layer's vector path so any extra white doesn't show outside the letters. Create a new layer called 'Highlights' with the blending mode set to Overlay. Now brush in white highlights, remembering where the light is meant to be coming from. ❯

BRUSHES: THE HARD OR SOFT OPTION?

❯ It's very easy to feel you can save time by using harder brushes. In reality, using a soft brush with 10% opacity and Shape Dynamics turned on will give you more realistic-looking results. It may take you twice as long, but in the end it will always look twice as good.

12 Next we'll need to add shadows. Select the 'Type' layer, duplicate it (**Cmd/Ctrl + J**), call the result 'Shadows' and move it to the top of the layer stack. Change its colour to C21, M35, Y56 and K6, and set the blending mode to Linear Burn (this will make all the type very dark, but don't worry as we're only applying it to the shadows).

Make a selection from this layer's vector path and, using the same brush as before, take time to paint on shadows in a direction opposite to that of the highlights.

13 Pop back into Illustrator and select the main type shape. Add a 1pt white stroke and copy and paste it into Photoshop as a Smart Object. Call this layer 'Glow'. Add a white Outer Glow via the Blending Options button in the Layers panel. Create a selection around the type again and erase most of this glow, leaving the extreme highlights as white.

14 Repeat the previous step, this time with thicker line settings that will work against the shadows coming off the main type.

15 In Illustrator, create a couple of strokes offset from the main element. To do this, select the main element and hit **Object > Path > Offset Path** with a positive offset value (try 3mm). Repeat this step with an offset value double your initial one.

These two results will be used as very subtle waves in the background, as if the type had been dropped into some milk. To achieve this effect, copy and paste them into Photoshop at the base of the layer stack, change their colour to white, then use Inner Shadow and Outer Glow in the Layer Style dialog to give them the look shown.

16 Now sit back and review the whole image. I usually spend some time at this point fixing details.

For example, the colours may be good, but still not as amazing as you feel they could be. To address this, add a Hue/Saturation adjustment layer at the very top of the layer stack. Set the Saturation to +40 and the Lightness to -5. This will give you a result that's look good enough to lick off a plate. ∎

Above top Art for a Canadian Bacardi Breezer advertising campaign.
Above centre An ad for Cadbury – it was while he was working on alternative versions of this ad that Radim had the idea for this tutorial.
Above One of a series of abstract patterns created for the packaging of Celebrity Elite hair products.

THE WORLD'S GREATEST CREATIVE MAGAZINE

Be inspired any time and anywhere

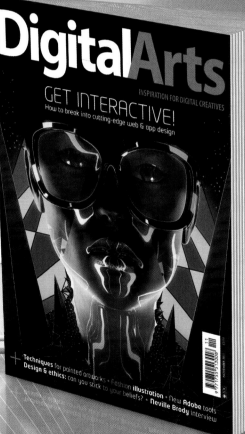

join the community

 twitter.com/digital_arts

 facebook.com/digitalartsmagazine

DigitalArts
INSPIRATION FOR DIGITAL CREATIVES

Online ● Print ● Mobile ● Digital

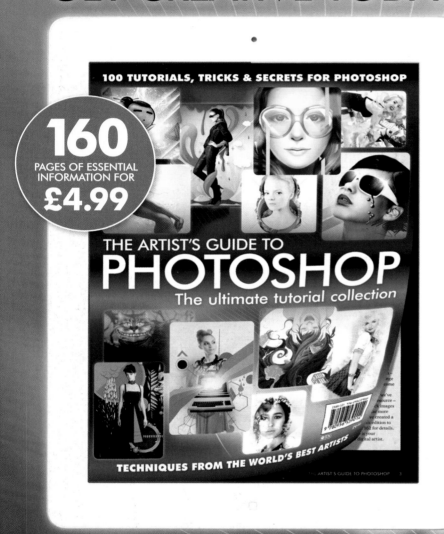